VINCENT DE PAUL
and
CHARITY

VINCENT DE PAUL
and
CHARITY

A Contemporary Portrait
of His Life and Apostolic Spirit

by
André Dodin, C.M.

translated by
Jean Marie Smith
and
Dennis Saunders

edited by
Hugh O'Donnell, C.M.
and
Marjorie Gale Hornstein

New City Press

In thanksgiving
for the zeal and joy
of the members of the
Congregation of the Mission
and
Daughters of Charity
in Ethiopia
the first to welcome this translation
as participants in the Vincentian Week
Addis Ababa, Ethiopia
October 19-24, 1992

New City Press, 86 Mayflower Ave., New Rochelle, NY 10801
©1993 New City Press
Printed in the United States of America

Cover picture: an early portrait of Vincent de Paul
by François Simon de Tours

Translated by Jean Marie Smith and Dennis Saunders
from the original French edition
St. Vincent de Paul et la charité
©1960 Editions de Seuil, Collection *Maîtres Spirituels*

Library of Congress Cataloging-in-Publication Data:

Dodin, André.
    [St. Vincent de Paul et la charité. English]
    Vincent de Paul and charity / André Dodin : translated
by Jean Marie Smith and Dennis Saunders, edited by Hugh O'Donnell
and Marjorie Gale Hornstein

    Includes bibliographical references.
    ISBN 1-56548-054-6 : $9.95
    1. Vincent de Paul, Saint, 1581-1660. 2. Christian saints
—France—Biography. 3. Vincentians—History—17th century.
I. O'Donnell, Hugh. II. Title.
BX4705.V6D63   1993
271'.7702—dc20 93-15188

Contents

Preface

An opportunity to read and reflect on the life of Saint Vincent at the Maison-Mère in Paris during the fall of 1987 led to an unexpected encounter with Father André Dodin, C.M. It was one of the special graces of my sabbatical year. I hadn't imagined I would have the opportunity to tap into his knowledge and love of Vincent. Eventually, to my surprise and satisfaction, I was able to ask him everything I wanted to know about Vincent and his spiritual journey. It was then that I read the present volume, *Saint Vincent de Paul et la Charité,* and discovered another perspective from which to understand Vincent. Father Dodin, in person and in his writings, was an excellent mentor.

The door to this new way of knowing Vincent was opened to me through confrontation. As an amateur (a non-professional who loved Vincent) I was in search of his secret. I hoped to penetrate it and acquire a confident grasp of his spirituality. I didn't intend to be an expert, but I longed for the expert's sure authority. It was then that I learned from Father Dodin that Vincent didn't have a spirituality and that anyone who desired to master Vincent's spirituality might examine himself for arrogance! That was the confrontation which opened the door for me. No, Vincent did not have a spirituality. He had a spiritual way. God, for Vincent, was found in experience, events, persons, circumstances, history, life, but not in a system of doctrines. His way was the way of experience, faith, and practical wisdom — all embraced in the spirit of love. Chapter 2, "His Spiritual Way," is the heart of the book and reveals Vincent's interiority in relation to history, circumstances and events.

A second insight concerned humility. Vincent's self-depre-

cating language and skeptical attitude toward human nature
had seemed exaggerated to me, perhaps even tinged with
Jansenism. It was difficult to square his attitude with the
goodness of creation and his immense love and compassion
for people. I began to understand Vincent's humility, however, in terms of a self-emptying which is correlative to being
filled with the Spirit of Jesus. Humility creates room for God's
unimpeded action in us. I do not claim this settles the question
of Vincent's apparent or real hardness on human nature, but
it opened a way to the immense liberating power of humility
in his life.

I also learned that Benet of Canfield, who was regarded as
the master of the masters of seventeenth-century French
spirituality, was Vincent's mentor concerning God's will.
Father André Duval gave Vincent a copy of Canfield's *Rule of
Perfection,*[1] when he first arrived in Paris in 1608. Canfield
believed the whole spiritual life was contained in the single
rule of doing the will of God. When I had the opportunity of
reading the *Rule of Perfection,* I experienced the meaning of
God's will for Vincent in a new way.

Canfield began with the External Will of God which is
revealed in the laws, commands and prohibitions that are part
of every life. The reality of God's will, then, proceeded in an
increasingly interior direction, which Canfield called the Interior Will of God, that is, the will of God as it is revealed
interiorly in our mind, heart, feelings and movements of the
spirit. Finally, there was the Supereminent Will of God which
is the knowledge of God's will arising from love and intimate
communion. Canfield showed that God's will is rooted in
love, which leads us beyond the extrinsicism that has often

---

1. See the critical edition: Jean Orcibal, *Benoit de Canfield: La Règle de
   Perfection, The Rule of Perfection* (Paris: Presses Universitaires de
   France, 1982). Canfield was an English Capuchin who wrote in both
   French and English. Though all three parts of his book are in French,
   only the first two parts are in English.

made God's will appear arbitrary and inhuman. God's will arises from God's very being and love welling up in the world and in the hearts of those who surrender to God. In short, Vincent, through Canfield, came to know "God is here!"

The goal of this translation has been to render Father Dodin's text as faithfully and completely as possible in keeping with the needs of an English-speaking audience. The French text is always available to those doing research or in need of the exact words of Father Dodin. The modifications of the text are as follows: the bibliography was updated, the section entitled "Disputed Questions" was condensed into two footnotes on the date of Vincent's birth and the captivity, and the section entitled "Chronology" was eliminated because it was not helpful for English-speaking readers. The section entitled "Problems Facing Vincent's Biographers" was edited to suit the changed historical perspective since Father Dodin first wrote in 1960.

I thank Jean Marie Smith and Dennis Saunders for the love for words and the love for Vincent they brought to the translation. I thank Marjorie Gale Hornstein for her abilities as an editor, her gift of clarity and her feeling for the mind and heart of Vincent. I thank Fred Eyerman for his support, encouragement and typing. It was teamwork that made it possible to render Dodin's classic French into contemporary English.

I thank John Rybolt, C.M., for his clear advice and ready guidance and all the members of the Vincentian Studies Institute who have encouraged this translation.

My thanks also go to Father Paul Gunth, C.M., who introduced me to Father Dodin in Paris, for his kindness to me as a father and brother.

Finally, I thank Father André Dodin as my mentor in the way of Vincent.

Hugh O'Donnell, C.M.

Introduction

We have no difficulty recognizing Vincent de Paul in his pictures and statues. He is a familiar and long-time friend to so many of us. Yet, the complex and intriguing nature of this man is easily overlooked, this man who modestly signed his name in the peasant fashion, Depaul, while his contemporaries called him Monsieur Vincent and we honor him today as Saint Vincent. We can easily forget the stages of his personal transformation. We may decide it is too difficult to plunge into the eight thousand pages of letters and conferences and, consequently, miss his carefully articulated teaching. We may separate him from the far-reaching effects upon the world of spiritual and charitable movements he set in motion, and leave ourselves with a two dimensional image of him.

Though I do not claim to have succeeded, my aim in this volume has been to discover and present a sharp and vibrant picture of Vincent for our time. My hope is that Vincent can be encountered:

- in the events of his earthly ministry;
- in the spiritual doctrine which nourished him;
- in the rich and wonderful tradition he inspired.

I welcome you to join me in this journey of discovery.

Vincent's Earthly Ministry

The Historical Setting and Spiritual Climate of His Times

Vincent de Paul was born in 1581[1] in the village of Pouy in the Landes of southern France during the reign of Henry III. He may have seen Henry IV, while living in Paris from 1608 to 1610. At any rate, he knew and associated with people of rank — Richelieu, Louis XIII (who asked for him when he was dying), Anne of Austria, Mazarin, Chancellor Seguier and those responsible for the education of Louis XIV. It was not until Louis XIV was ready to take charge of the destinies of France that Vincent died on September 27, 1660.

France was not as we know it today. Henry IV's kingdom consisted of seventy-two of the ninety *départéments* in present-day France. Foreign enclaves such as Venaissin, Nivernais and Flanders interrupted the kingdom's unity.

The population, despite the large number of children, often ten or twelve to a family, was stable. France's population fluctuated between 17 and 20 million. Migration was rare. Wars, epidemics and famines ravaged the towns. As many as fifty percent of the children died in infancy. Adults lived

---

1. For two and a half centuries biographers peacefully affirmed that Vincent was born in 1576. In this they followed Abelly, who did not have Vincent's birth certificate and assumed Vincent was of proper age when he was ordained to the priesthood in 1600. In 1922, Pierre Coste, as he edited the complete works of Vincent, demonstrated that Vincent was born in 1581. He based his conclusion on the internal evidence of Vincent's own words found in his letters. Today José Maria Roman has argued that Vincent was born a year earlier in 1580. See his *San Vicente de Paul: I, Biographia* (Madrid, 1981), 30-31.

twenty or twenty-five years on the average. Only members of the well-nourished middle class might hope to survive to their mid-forties.

Food was scarce. Meat was a luxury, livestock meager. Vegetables, soup and bread were dietary staples. Peasants subsisted on bread made from mixed grains. The middle and upper classes enjoyed wheat or rye breads. The soil suffered from lack of nutrients and fields lay fallow every other year. Lack of transportation crippled the distribution of farm produce. Epidemics and famines could wipe out as many as thirty to forty percent of the population in the provinces.

Holy wars were the scourge of rural areas, and the wounds they caused would not be healed. A reporter-illustrator of the time chronicled the horrifying results of these wars. The major conflicts of Lorraine, Picardy and Champagne as well as lesser known battles left the population disorganized, impoverished and paralyzed. Confusion and agitation ruled Lorraine even before the Fronde[2] reached the capital. In 1633, the peasants of Lyons plundered the customs offices. In 1634, the people of Rouen sacked the house of tax collectors. In 1639, the dyers and drapers of Rouen assaulted the house of Le Tellier who collected the salt tax. Louis XIII and Richelieu sent four thousand troops to Marshal Gassion to bring Caen and Rouen to submission. Normandy remained under siege by the Va-nu-piéds,[3] while the other provinces continued to be agitated by unrest.

Undernourished, abused, frustrated and illiterate — the people had little hope for anything better. Only one out of four men and one out of ten women could read or write. Shifting economic and cultural tides led to sudden upheavals

2. The Fronde was an uprising against Cardinal Mazarin during Louis XIV's early years (1648-52) due to his unpopularity and financial demands.
3. Va-nu-piéds means bare-footed. It refers to a rebel army determined to abolish all taxes levied since Henry IV. The movement was led by Jean Va-nu-piéds, possibly a fictitious name used to designate the revolt as an uprising of the poor.

of opinion. Within weeks, entire families and villages abandoned Catholicism or abjured Protestantism. Itinerant prophets and false messiahs stirred villages, aroused passions and then were soon forgotten. Crises aroused suspicions of witchcraft. Among the common folk a belief in the marvelous was paradoxically coupled with fear of diabolical possession. There was a fascination with all unexplained phenomena. In spite of it all, France's rural population remained steadfast in faith. Moral laws, the necessities of life and political pressures exerted a force which produced equilibrium.

Very gradually, the new social profile of France began to take shape. The nobility, the first estate of the nation, was weakened by factions and decimated by the loss of as many as 220 members each year in duels. France's economy steadily declined. As the powerful grip of the monarchy also declined, it sought to shore up its fortunes with further financial claims. Richelieu passionately spent his energies attempting to restore prosperity. He called for national solidarity. He was inspired and seduced by the prosperity of Spain, England and Holland to promote commerce and the navy. France was emerging as a middle class, capitalist commercial nation after having been an agrarian, feudal state. Richelieu, as Victor Tapié mentions, succeeded in releasing France from her medievalism and led her to new horizons.

The Catholic clergy, the second estate in France, was the country's great landowner. Two-thirds of all territory belonged to them. The Catholic clergy generously financed the religious wars. The power of this group included 123 bishoprics, at least 152,000 churches and chapels and 4,000 convents. In 1660, it was estimated that there were 256,000 ecclesiastics and 181,000 men and women religious in France.

The emergence and rapid progress of Protestantism worried clerical authorities and the spiritually-minded. Within only fifty years the reformed religion claimed one million followers and seven hundred houses of worship in France and had established centers to train its ministers in the Academies

of several major cities. The offensive of the new faith became
more serious as the clergy suffered from the capricious abuses
of the *commende*, a form of absentee administration. Eight
hundred and fifteen abbeys and 280 priories were administered *in absentia* by people whose primary interest was
material advancement and wealth. The king nominated bishops, often young and immature, who had little power to
enforce or bring about necessary changes within the diocese.
Reform depended on the ministry of reliable parish priests.
Yet, a sizeable number of priests remained uneducated and
mediocre. Vincent de Paul, Adrien Bourdoise, Jean-Jacques
Olier and Saint-Cyran[4] believed that it was the priests who
were responsible for the state of the Church. How, under
such conditions, could the faith be effectively preserved?

Social structures were solid and remained that way. Certain
elite groups which came into being at the beginning of the
century and well-known abbesses established networks of
influence. Their activity, more unified than during the League
days,[5] became a solidifying element in the social structure. In
spite of opposition from the Estates-General[6] (1614), Parlement (1626) and Louis XIII (1629), approximately one hundred convents were established in Paris between 1598 and
1648. The Church, even though badly wounded, kept its
vitality and continued to give life.

A new danger paradoxically compelled a regrouping of
moral forces. Free-thinking, the ubiquitous secret of the sixteenth century, was now insolently in the open. It worried
those in power, scandalized the common folk and incensed
those who were spiritually-minded. "There are fifty thousand

---

4. As the abbot of Saint-Cyran, Jean Du Vergier de Hauranne became
   known as Saint-Cyran.
5. The League was a confederation of Catholics formed at the end of the
   sixteenth century to defend the Catholic faith from the Calvinists and
   overthrow Henry II, in order to place the leader of the confederation on
   the throne of France.
6. The legislative assembly in France before the Revolution.

atheists in Paris," lamented Father Mersenne, undoubtedly a victim of his frightened imagination. What did it matter! Ever since Theophile de Viau's lawsuit (1623), the royal authorities had been alerted. The vision of the Church retreating from the West periodically haunted many. Angelique Arnaud, Saint-Cyran, Francis de Sales, the Bishop of Geneva, and Saint Vincent de Paul wondered about the future of Catholic Europe. The wise and discreet Vincent occasionally expressed the thought that within 100 or 150 years the Church might cease to exist in this part of the world. Such thoughts stimulated his zeal for the missions to non-believers.

The task was immense. Rural areas were not in a position to benefit at that time from the admirable efforts of Pierre de Bérulle and the contemplatives. The new religious congregations certainly worked with unstinting courage. The Jesuits in Paris shepherded at least two thousand students at Clermont College. The Capuchins preached and gave missions untiringly. Teaching communities such as the Ursulines grew up and developed. Religious literature, which took pains to address the decaying moral condition, was circulated widely. The *Introduction to the Devout Life* by Francis de Sales and *The Interior Occupation of a Devout Soul* by Father Coton were popular. *The Imitation of Christ* was printed once or twice yearly and *The Spiritual Combat*, which Francis de Sales quoted often, was adopted by all fervent souls. Despite such efforts, common folks were often abandoned and preyed upon by Reformers. Vincent de Paul was quick to declare that the people were perishing in ignorance and misery. It was for these abandoned people that he felt he was born. When he became aware of his vocation, we don't know. In any case, it was toward them he advanced — taking a few detours on the way.

The Evolution of His Conscience

A Time of Seeking

Vincent's journey on earth lasted eighty years. His first undertakings were tentative, anxious and groping. It took him thirty-six years to develop that assurance which gave shape and character to his unforgettable face.

Vincent was the third child of Jean de Paul and Bertrande Demoras, a peasant couple with six children. Contemporary paintings effectively introduce us into a typical peasant house—no elegance, few comforts, no misery. People and objects were well matched. The pictures, however, fail to show the labors and sorrows of the characters. Whether a scene depicts the celebration of a baptism or a midday break, the same atmosphere of hard work is evident and reflected in the people's faces. "Where I come from," Vincent stated later, "we eat millet grain cooked in a pot; at meal times it is placed in a soup bowl and all those at home gather to eat it before going back to work" (IX, 84).[7]

As a child, Vincent saw in the face of the peasant woman who was his mother an ineffable love. It was from this woman that he received inspiration to ground his future work in a radical and passionate love for poor people and those in need. As a young man, he was animated by the heart of this woman whom God and nature caused him to cherish more than all the queens in the world. He later was able to mobilize the unsuspected resources and incredible affectivity of seventeenth century women. Madame de Gondi, Louise de Marillac, the Ladies and Daughters of Charity were neither mysterious nor idealized human beings. They were souls called to give

---

7. Roman numerals designate the volume and Arabic numbers the pages of Pierre Coste's edition of Vincent's works: *Saint Vincent de Paul, Correspondance, Entretiens, Documents* (Paris: Gabalda, 1920-25).

themselves to God and to others in a supernatural blossoming of maternal genius.

In a house where everyone worked, the young worked too. Young Vincent was responsible for shepherding the pigs and lambs. "I went to keep the herds of pigs," he liked to declare and thus humble himself before those who thought themselves important. He handled the shafts of the wooden plow and as seasons changed, led herds to the Chalosse plains or as far away as Saint-Sever, a distance of nearly sixty kilometers. Years later, this general of the Mission and member of the Regency Council did not hesitate to return to his profession of herder and, despite the harsh winter and poor travelling conditions, led two horses and 240 sheep from the besieged farm of Orsigny (III, 412). In the twilight of his life, Vincent remembered his shepherd days when he slept behind hedges or in the shelter of a thicket and longed to retire to the hollow of a bush. "I simply have to tell you," he confided to one of his Missionaries, "that in the midst of my infirmities there is a great desire to be able to work in some rustic village and I believe I would indeed be happy if God granted me this grace" (V, 203-04).

In 1595, Vincent's father recognized Vincent's talents and enrolled him in the boarding school at Dax with the Franciscans. Monsieur de Comet, the Judge of Pouy, also a presidial lawyer at the Dax Court, took an interest in the young man. He entrusted Vincent with the education of his children and guided him toward the priesthood. To the rural people, ecclesiastical life was the normal path to rapid improvement of one's lot in life. The young man, to whom his father's rustic appearance was once an embarrassment, telescoped his studies in humanities into a single year. He also claimed to be forever a high school student, but his proficiency in Latin won him admission to Toulouse University. In 1596, he received tonsure and minor orders at Bidache. The impatient youngster from Gascony was admitted to holy orders and ordained to the priesthood on September 23, 1600 by the old bishop of Perigueux, Francis de Bourdeilles. "Had I known as I know

now," he later confided, "what entering the priesthood meant, I think I would never have had the temerity to receive holy orders and would have preferred to till the land rather than enter such an awesome state" (V, 368; VII, 463). Some time later, he celebrated his first Mass at Buzet.

He was then in a position to ask for a benefice.[8] The Bishop of Dax offered him the pastorate of Tilh, but when a more persistent candidate challenged him for it, Vincent discreetly withdrew. Rome attracted him and in the jubilee year his pilgrimage there provided an opportunity to see his holiness, Pope Clement VIII. Vincent was delighted and moved by the tomb of the apostles. On his return to France he continued his studies. His funds were low, so to improve the state of his finances he accepted boarding students at Buzet and later took them to the university city. While looking after them, he earned a bachelor's degree in theology. Fortune was smiling upon him and he had hopes of receiving at his young age . . . a bishopric.

The death of an elderly woman from Toulouse made him heir to four or five hundred crowns. In order to collect his legacy, he was compelled to pursue a man of doubtful character who was in debt to the woman's estate. The debtor, a merchant, described as a "real rogue who was good at business," had gone to Marseilles. In pursuit of the man, Vincent found himself without money and decided to sell his rented horse. Vincent probably, so it is assumed, repaid the horse's owner when he got his money. Eventually, he had the man imprisoned and received three hundred crowns. To save money, Vincent returned to Toulouse via Narbonne. He boarded a ship and mysteriously disappeared.

He was neither seen nor heard from for two years. To explain his mysterious absence, he told of an incredible adventure which took him from the European scene. It was

---

8. A benefice is an ecclesiastical post to which property or a determined revenue is attached.

a completely singular odyssey. He had been in Barbary, he explained to Monsieur de Comet. Captured by pirates, he had been taken to the North coast of Africa and sold successively into the service of four different masters. The first, a fisherman, the second an alchemist, the third the alchemist's nephew and finally an apostate from the Christian faith. Vincent succeeded in escaping from Tunis with his last master and crossed the Mediterranean in a skiff. From Aigues-Mortes they travelled to Avignon. The apostate, choked by tears, abjured his errors before the Vice-Legate of Avignon, Bishop Francis Montorio.

What, we wonder, was the reaction of Monsieur de Comet to this lost page of Vincent's story which sounded like something from *The Tale of the Thousand and One Nights*? On the other hand, we can well imagine how the ordeal of a two-year absence from Europe must have tested the physical and moral stamina of our cadet from Gascony. At any rate, his journey is easier to follow from this point forward.[9]

No sooner had he completed recounting his misfortune to the Vice-Legate than the two left Avignon for Rome. Vincent

---

9. (*Editor's Note:* What follows is a condensation of Dodin's exposition of this question, which in the original French is found in an appendix entitled "Disputed Questions.") The debate concerning the historicity of Vincent's captivity in Algiers flared up in 1927 following the publication of the definitive edition of Vincent's letters and conferences by Pierre Coste. Those who believed the captivity was an historical event relied on the honesty of Vincent, the absence of contrary historical evidence, the hypothetical nature of the opposite opinion, and the evident knowledge of medicine and alchemy that Vincent possessed and demonstrated in the letter. Those who suspected or denied the captivity's actual occurrence appealed to Vincent's lifelong silence about these events, or pointed to the unlikelihood of the details (for example, crossing six hundred miles of the Mediterranean in a skiff), or finally noted significant parallels to literature, for example, to *The Illustrious Don Quixote of La Mancha*. André Dodin is himself content to point out that Vincent was a Gascon and is best understood in terms of the poetry and song and love of enchantment of the peasantry of southern France.

for the second time entered the Eternal City and was received by a high-ranking member of the Church. While pursuing his studies he closely observed the Italian spirit with its rhythmical, relaxed tempo, so different from the frenzied pace of the French. Rome, however, was not Vincent's kind of place. He felt he would be better off in France and was attracted to Paris. He arrived in the capital in September, 1608.

This city is another world
A flourishing world within
Brimming with people and with goods
Overflowing with everything.

Paris is the only city in the world where life is lived fully. "Anywhere else," says John de Jandun, "people only live relatively." Vincent paused in the suburb of Saint-Germain, encountered a compatriot and, unable to find other suitable lodging, remained with him. Vincent was not long in discovering that this was not to become his home. A pharmacist who delivered medicine to the bedridden Vincent took advantage of the absence of Vincent's roommate, a judge, and stole the judge's money. Vincent, unaware of the crime, was accused of theft. Threatened with harm and evicted from the apartment, Vincent moved to a house in the rue de Seine, over which hung the seal of Saint Nicholas.

Eventually our young man from Gascony found lodging with the chaplains of Queen Marguerite. Living so close to royal splendor, however, did not enrich him in any way. He hoped his appointment to the Abbey of Saint Leonard-de-Chaumes by the Archbishop of Aix would help his finances. But when he went to take possession of it, he found it in ruins. He incurred debt and signed promissory note after promissory note.

Fortunately, his spiritual friends helped him keep his head above water. Vincent was on good terms with Pierre de Bérulle and often visited with the future members of the Oratory. Guided by this leader of the French school and spiritual director of the elite, Vincent tried to find light for his path. Bérulle observed him and tried to decipher his soul, but remained unsure. Vincent asked questions of Bérulle, prayed and examined himself. He chose not to join the Oratory, but accepted the pastorate of Clichy at Bérulle's invitation to replace Father Bourgoing, who had chosen to enter the new community. For the first time, twelve years after his priestly ordination, Vincent had the privilege of being a shepherd of souls. In this canonical appointment, he was at last able to fully exercise his role as priest.

Clichy

On May 12, 1612 the young priest Vincent took charge of the semi-rural parish of six hundred souls. His ministry brought him much happiness as he ministered in the pulpit and confessional and at the baptismal font, repaired and decorated the church, initiated the Confraternity of the Rosary, assembled candidates for the priesthood and catechized both children and adults. Everything he did met with success. He told the Bishop of Paris, "I have such good and obedient parishioners that I often think that no one could be happier than I, not you, your excellency, not even his holiness the pope" (IX, 646).

At the de Gondis

Vincent left Clichy to become tutor to the eldest sons of the illustrious Philippe-Emmanuel de Gondi and his wife Françoise Marguerite de Silly. We can only assume that Pierre de Bérulle was still not sure where Vincent's vocation would lead, but realized that Clichy was not a permanent position for him. Wanting to place him in higher positions, he encouraged him to accept the assignment from de Gondi, a man who was handsome, worldly, wealthy and the General of the Royal Galleys.

By 1613, Philippe-Emmanuel de Gondi had acquired several

titles. As the nephew of Archbishop Pierre de Gondi of Paris, his many acquaintances included priests and religious. The archbishop died in 1616 and was succeeded by Henri de Gondi. On August 3, 1622, he in turn died while accompanying the king to Beziers and was succeeded by Jean François de Gondi. Two of his aunts were Dominican Sisters in Poissy and one, Louise, was prioress of the Convent. Philippe-Emmanuel de Gondi was a man who circulated a lot. From the rue des Petits-Champs in Paris he oversaw his lands in Picardy, Burgundy and Champagne. Jean-François-Paul, his third son, was born September 2, 1613. He was destined to become the famous coadjutor bishop.

Vincent had been selected to guide the education of Pierre, fourteen, and Henri, seven. As he occupied this position of trust he found in castle life "the honest retirement" he had long been looking for.

Fortunately or unfortunately, he couldn't settle in there. At age thirty-two and in the prime of his life, he didn't have a full-time occupation. He had come to resemble a controversial theologian, also in "retirement," whom he had encountered at Queen Marguerite's palace. This fellow, having very little to do, was devoured by doubts and obsessed by scruples. "Land which has for some time lain fallow produces thistles and thorns" (XI, 33). Informed of the theologian's plight, Vincent undertook to help him. He advised him to find something to do, to lead an active life and to visit the poor. When his advice proved useless, Vincent decided to act. In a burst of generosity he offered to God to take upon himself the temptations of the theologian. The bargain struck, the afflicted theologian was totally delivered but Vincent now became burdened, worried and consumed by doubts. His spirit tumbled into darkness. It was an interior night for him.

When the de Gondis travelled, Vincent took advantage of the opportunity and followed his own advice. He sought opportunities for ministry. He taught catechism. He also evangelized the servants and peasant-farmers on Madame de

Gondi's estates. Madame de Gondi herself sought his advice and he became her spiritual director.

The Experiences of Folleville and Chatillon (1617)

It was in the course of a journey with the de Gondis that the light broke through and the struggle which he had endured for three or four years finally came to an end. At last Vincent understood that he must think of his future as a continual service of the poor. He understood that God must occupy and reign in his life, that he must not seek his own interest, but seek to perform the works of God. "It is necessary to seek God first, to look to God first of all. Let us seek the kingdom of God and everything besides will be given us. If we do God's works, he will take care of ours." The theocentric instructions of Bérulle took on flesh in a mystique of service to the poor. In the middle of the winter of 1617 at the bedside of an impoverished peasant, God gave Vincent a sign which filled him with a sense of certitude and peace.

It was at Gannes, near Folleville, where a peasant lay dying. At the peasant's deathbed, Vincent attentively listened to the confession of this man who had struggled for years with pride and been silenced by shame. It prevented him from confessing his sins to a priest. To Madame de Gondi he said, "Without this confession, Madame, I would have been damned!" Free at last, the dying peasant was at peace.

Taken aback by the admission of a man believed by all to be devout, the wife of the General of the Galleys saw the enormity of the evil. She turned to her spiritual director and said, "Monsieur Vincent, how many souls are lost in this way? What can we do?"

There was only one solution. Vincent methodically organized general confessions. On January 25, Vincent spoke on this subject to the parishioners of Folleville. For several days, aided by other priests, he pursued the work of the mission and discovered "his mission." We can imagine the days and months which followed. Vincent visited the peasants of the de Gondi lands, called them to the renewal of their consciences, preached and reconciled them in the sacrament.

Unfortunately, all was not that simple. Vincent had found his role but had not yet found his place. By June 8, 1617, with full knowledge that his path to God must pass among the poor, Vincent opened his troubled conscience to Bérulle and pondered whether or not to leave the de Gondi household. Bérulle, still unable to discern Vincent's destiny, listened to his arguments, agreed with them and backed his wishes. He suggested Vincent go to Chatillon-les-Dombes, a small parish near Lyons. This troubled parish, neglected by its six canons, all of them Counts of Saint John of Lyons, was in danger of falling into Protestant hands. Vincent immediately accepted the assignment and on August 1, 1617 was officially installed as pastor.

The Parish of Chatillon-les-Dombes (1617)

There events began to escalate. On his arrival Vincent sized up the task God had given him. He could not depend upon the indifferent chaplains, so he recruited Father Louis Girard from Lyons as his assistant. "One Sunday in August," he tells us, "as I was vesting for holy Mass, Madame de la Chassaigne came to tell me that in an isolated house one-quarter league away everyone was sick and needed help. My heart was deeply moved" (IX, 243). Emotion prompted him in his sermon to speak "miraculous" words, as he had in Folleville. After vespers, he and a good man of the parish visited the ailing family. He heard confessions and offered communion to the sick. Yet, he was perplexed. The generosity of the parishioners at that moment was great, but what would happen in the days and months ahead. "See how great their charity is," he said, "but it is poorly organized."

Vincent set to work. He gathered the women who were eager to be of service and by 23 August presented the first draft of the rules for their association. "When the Mother of God is invoked and taken as patroness of important matters, how could anything not go well and not bring glory to Jesus, her son" (XIV, 126). Building on this first draft, Vincent presented a new rule within three months.

The rules were a masterpiece of tenderness and organization. Everything was foreseen, from the ways of assisting and feeding the sick to locating resources and keeping the books. They gave guidance on how to "charitably invite the sick to eat for the love of Jesus and of his holy Mother." A certain order was to be followed. The first to be aided were the poor people who had someone with them. Those who were alone were to be attended to last, so that more time could be spent with them.

On November 24, 1617, Lord Mechatin Lafalye, the Vicar General of Lyons, approved the rule and on December 8, 1617, the feast of the Immaculate Conception, Vincent proceeded with the solemn erection of the Confraternity of Charity in the chapel of the hospital.

Return to Paris

Vincent's failure to secure the permission of the de Gondis in leaving their employ unleashed intense distress at his defection. He had departed from the household with an explanation that he must take a trip, and later in a letter begged for their forgiveness. A coalition was formed to obtain his return to Paris. It included Cardinal de Bérulle, who gently pleaded with him. Pained, Vincent gave in and headed back to the capital.

In no more than five months the entire character of the parish had been renewed. Three programs were under way in the new Chatillon: evangelization through charitable works, regular celebration of the sacraments, and ministry to the poor as the special friends of Jesus. A firm foundation for the renewed parish was in place. On December 23, Vincent knocked at the door of de Bérulle and on Christmas Eve rejoined the de Gondi household.

His Major Foundations (1618-33)

Whether he knew it or not, Vincent's life was entering a new stage. Now that his vision of the future was transformed, he had to go forward. He followed divine Providence step by step, according to the *Rule of Perfection* of Benet of Canfield, which his friend and mentor, André Duval, praised so highly. He was devoted to always honoring Providence and "not treading on its heels." Now that the intimate depths of his being were engaged in the service of the poor, the next step was to insure the order and continuity of his mission. He needed, therefore, to establish the institutions which would permit him to achieve his work and make the mission of Jesus available to others in the future.

Meeting Francis de Sales

Vincent was no longer alone. In 1618 and again in 1619, he met Francis de Sales, whom he regarded as the concrete image of the goodness of God. "How good must God be," he often said, "since the Bishop of Geneva is so good." A few meetings had been enough to knit a solid friendship between them. Vincent admired the perfect equilibrium of the author of *The Introduction to the Devout Life*, and confided to him his worries about religious life and the sanctification of the laity in and through secular life. Together they longed for a profound reform of the clergy and a simplified form of preaching which would feed hungry souls. A spirit of cooperation grew between them which led Vincent to become the spiritual father to the Parisian Visitation Nuns and for a few years the spiritual director of Jane Frances de Chantal. After Francis' death, Vincent continued in this role and quite unconsciously imbibed Salesian doctrines and practices.

Companions

Others gathered around Vincent, whose presence was an encouragement and support to him. These priests were also friends of the poor and of God. Father de Bérulle, busy with the Oratory, somehow lost interest in Vincent and at times even appeared hostile toward him. It didn't matter. Two dynamic and authoritative teachers, whom Vincent met at de Bérulle's, were his allies. The first was André Duval, the royal professor of theology at the Sorbonne. Vincent venerated him as his teacher. It was the modest, discreet, confident and holy Monsieur Duval who enabled Vincent to recognize his call to establish a community and later accept the huge priory of Saint-Lazare.

The other, Jean du Vergier de Hauranne (Saint-Cyran), was a compatriot, a friend with whom Vincent had some common financial interests. They discussed the problems of the Church and the priesthood and needed reforms. Their friendship was without a cloud for twelve years. Vincent recognized, however, that he and his friend were not on the same path, when Richelieu imprisoned the Director of Port-Royal. Vincent nevertheless did not hesitate to testify in favor of his old friend before the ecclesiastical judge, Monsieur Lescot, even at the risk of unsettling the dreaded Cardinal-Minister (March 31-April 2, 1639; XIII, 86-93).

It helps to call to mind the attitude of Madame de Gondi, if we wish to recreate the climate of these years. Full of joy with the return of the father of her soul, she supported his undertakings with her heart and soul and underwrote the costs.

It was under these favorable conditions that Vincent created his essential works: the Mission and the Charities.

Emergence of the Mission

Vincent's flock was growing considerably. Philippe-Emmanuel de Gondi entrusted to him the prisons and galleys and petitioned Louis XIII to appoint him the General Chaplain of the Galleys (February 8, 1619). Vincent immediately visited his impoverished parishioners in Paris and Marseilles (1622). He conducted a mission for them at Bordeaux on the galleys in 1623.

He took advantage of being close to home and extended his trip to include Dax. There he bade a final farewell to his family.

Vincent could no longer question his mission: the poor were his masters. He was at their disposition and had to obey them. During a mission at Montmirail and Marchais (1621-22), a Protestant refuted all Vincent's arguments and confronted him on his own terms, saying "the Church of Christ cannot abandon the poor, but . . . there are ten thousand priests in Paris, while the poor in the rural areas remain lost in their appalling ignorance" (XI, 34). Two retreats, one in Soissons and the other in Valprofonde, irrevocably convinced Vincent of his vocation to the poor. It was now only a matter of establishing a solid and stable institution.

Vincent received his degree in canon law and was thus able to be appointed Principal of the College des Bons-Enfants (March 1, 1624) where residential quarters were put at his disposal. On April 17, 1625 Philippe-Emmanuel de Gondi and his wife, Françoise, signed a contract endowing Vincent's mission with forty-five thousand livres (XIII, 197-202). Madame de Gondi died on June 23, 1625, as if her life's purpose had been the signing of this document. As in Chatillon, the foundation was laid. The Archbishop of Paris approved the Congregation of the Mission on April 24, 1626, and soon after Vincent took the first steps to obtain approval from Rome.

Clouds Over Paris and Rome

From 1626 to 1628 the fate of the Mission hung in the balance. Monsieur de Gondi had joined the Oratory and intended to withdraw his endowment of the Mission. Although Saint-Cyran dissuaded him, the close call alarmed and frightened the infant missionary band. In Rome, opposition from Cardinal de Bérulle was evident and approval of the little Company was twice denied (August 22 and September 25) by the Roman Congregations.

Responsibility to the Clergy

In spite of opposition from his foes, Vincent remained steadfast in his purpose and continued the missions. He asked himself what God wanted him to do. If people easily went over to Protestantism, as in Chatillon, was it not because of the ignorance of the pastors responsible for their instruction? To be fair, to what degree was the clergy responsible for being without formation and bogged down in ignorance? Madame de Gondi's encounter with a priest who did not know the rite of absolution was not unusual, which Vincent himself was able to confirm from experience. Yet, without priests, nothing could be done in the Church. The future of Christianity depended upon the priests. This was the conviction of Bourdoise, Saint-Cyran and of Vincent himself.

The Retreat at Beauvais

Would it be possible to reform priests who had benefices and were hardened by laziness? No one would dream of it. There was only one thing to do — select eager candidates to the priesthood and insure them solid instruction. Bishop Potier of Beauvais favored the plan and in July, 1628, while meeting with Vincent and sharing with him his concerns, invited him to come in September to preach the retreat to the ordinands. The retreat was a great success and the formula was immediately adopted in Paris. Soon retreats for ordinands multiplied to such a degree they eclipsed those for ecclesiastics. The prior of the Convent of Saint-Lazare-lès-Paris and the Archbishop of Paris were thinking of the importance of ordinands when in 1632 they allowed Vincent and the Missionaries to occupy the vast priory. One blessing followed on another, and early in 1633 Rome approved the Congregation of the Mission with the Bull *Salvatoris Nostri* mentioning ordinands as a principal work of the Mission.

A Decisive Turn

Events took a decisive turn, unforeseen by Vincent. It was Vincent's way to befriend events, by which God led him by the hand. God was now associating him with the radical task of Catholic reform. He worked with Cardinal de La Rochefoucauld, who had already entrusted the case concerning visionaries to him (September 1630). The future of the mission to the poor was also secured for him. From now on, in spite of his natural inclination to circumspection, Vincent took large strides forward.

In 1633, he drew up a rule for an association of priests which soon brought the elite of Parisian clergy together at Saint Lazare. Each Tuesday they gathered to pray, work, reflect and encourage each other. By 1660, the Tuesday Conferences of Paris had 250 participants. Among them, twenty-two were eventually called to the episcopate. Bossuet, among many others, prided himself as disciple of the one who spoke like an oracle of God. This company of the Tuesday Conferences also conducted missions. Vincent used them everywhere: in 1633, at the Hospital of Quinze-Vingts; in 1638, at the court at Saint-Germain-en-Laye; in 1639, at the Hôtel-Dieu; in 1641 and 1642, in the suburb of Saint-Germain; in 1657, at the General Hospital for the poor; and in 1657, at the invitation of Anne of Austria for a general mission in Metz.

Development of the Charities

In the years 1617-33, the Charities experienced a miraculous springtime. For sixteen years Vincent patiently observed people, studied ways and means of doing things and experimented with formulas.

After Chatillon, his only thought had been to preach in all the parishes of Madame de Gondi and establish at the end of each mission a charitable organization as had been done at Chatillon. He accomplished this. Believing everyone was entitled to do something, Vincent invited men to form Charities. The results, however, led Vincent to abandon Charities made up of men as well as those made up of both men and women and concentrate on perfecting the Charities run by women.

He soon noticed that the Charities could not be exclusively for poor sick people. In Macon it was necessary to respond to the situation of beggars (1621), and in Paris visiting the prisoners and the galley slaves quickly became the responsibility of specific Charities. It was necessary that the organization and formula of the Charities remain open. There came to be Charities for young indigent couples and Charities for victims of famine and war. In 1640, the Charities of Lorraine became centers of relief, food depots and refuges for women and religious exposed to soldiers' rudeness. We do not choose the poor, it is they who choose us.

Nevertheless, everywhere, in Paris as well as in Macon, time revealed two weaknesses that had to be corrected. If the Charities were to be effective, they required supervision and personal involvement. The heartfelt interest and good will of the ladies of nobility were no longer sufficient for the physical toil required in caring for the sick and cleaning and attending to the needs of the poor. Yet, it remained necessary to love one's neighbor as God — with the strength of one's arms and sweat of one's brow. Some of the Ladies of Charity had taken to delegating their work to their servants. Hired devotion was not enough; what was needed was a heart, a soul and unconditional, unbroken fidelity.

Louise de Marillac (1591-1660)

The one who was destined to join Vincent in directing this enterprise was Mademoiselle Legras. Her background, however, did not appear to prepare her for this undertaking. Born Louise de Marillac in 1591, she entered Vincent's life in 1624 as quietly as a shadow. No more than five feet tall, nervous and impressionable, she came from the illustrious Marillac family. She had never known her mother and lost her father when she was thirteen years old. Her confessor had dissuaded her from joining the Capuchin order and Louise married Antoine Legras. They had a son, Michel, who never ceased to be a source of worry to her. Her spiritual directors had advised her to be simple and cheerful and to come into possession of herself. Shortly after the death of Antoine, she opened her heart to Vincent, who offered the same advice.

The First Daughter of Charity

Not yet aware of Louise's talents, Vincent reluctantly assumed responsibility for the soul of this woman who had a delicate and worrying conscience. He soon, however, discovered the remarkable depths of her spirit and what she had to offer to the poor. Louise de Marillac took the place of Madame de Gondi, and, in many ways reminded Vincent of his earlier disciple. She evidenced the same fervor in heeding his advice, for example, when he asked her to be happy, love God, guard against self, renounce self-centeredness or discipline her imagination and impressions. "Be happy, honor the inactivity and the hidden state of the Son of God, accept paradoxical events, adore Providence, follow it, do not tread on its heels. . . . Our Lord is in continual communion with those who are united to his will and his non-will." This pastoral approach full of Salesian gentleness wisely combined the necessity for union with the divine will, promoted by Benet of Canfield, with the Augustinian perspectives so dear to de

Bérulle. The results were extraordinary. By 1629 under Vincent's guidance Louise de Marillac had become the first Daughter of Charity.

He sent her on an inspection tour of the Charities. With his clear guidance, Louise de Marillac discerned, inspired, accounted, suggested. She and Vincent saw that the Ladies of the Charities could not perform works at others' homes that they did not do in their own homes. So, Louise recruited reliable workers from the countryside, young women who were willing to serve the poor and devote themselves to God.

The Daughters of Charity

On November 29, 1633, a small house in the Saint Victor suburb became the birthplace of the Company of the Daughters of Charity, servants of the sick poor. They were to be religious without habits, veils or solemn vows. Vincent combined the perspectives of religious life with the vocation of missionary servants. He described their vocation in these unforgettable words:

> They will have for a monastery the houses of the sick and the house where their superior lives. For a cell, a rented room. For a chapel, the parish church. For a cloister, the streets of the city. For an enclosure, obedience. For a grate, the fear of God. For a veil, holy modesty. For profession, continual confidence in Providence and the offering of all that they are. (X, 661)

In order to insure abiding solidarity with the poor, whom misery never leaves alone, they would be the professed of Jesus living unceasingly among the poor.

This division of roles and functions allowed the Ladies to continue their assistance and presence. The Charities found new momentum. Paris adopted the formula and most of the Parisian parishes came to have sisters. The result was that well-to-do and middle-class families were associated with the work and the lives of poor servants. A permanent way was opened up for people to understand and help each other and to associate with one another in doing good. The Charities in practice lowered social barriers and fostered remarkable relationships among women of different rank.

National Activity (1633-43)

The religious foundations of Monsieur Vincent began to grow. Their diversity and size attracted attention. The originality and meaning of his enterprises developed in relationship to the political and religious circumstances of his time. There is always a temptation to separate Vincent's initiatives from what was going on, but he was a man of his time and willingly participated in the order and organization which surrounded him and of which he was part.

Richelieu, in spite of constant threats, remained in power and step by step erected the social and economic structures which transformed the nation.

Like Richelieu, but in another domain and with a different style, Vincent governed and organized. Yet, people remarked on his evenness of spirit. "Vincent is always Vincent," they said. His pursuit of the works of charity had four principal centers: the Mission, the Daughters of Charity, the Ladies of Charity and the religious of the Visitation.

The Mission

As the structure of the Mission developed during the years 1635-43, it seemed to be the personification of its founder. Vincent wanted the Mission to be different from the Oratory, larger in scope than the Saint Nicholas Community and of a different spirit than the Community of the Blessed Sacrament. He recognized that Monsieur Olier had a special vocation. Vincent himself was slowly becoming more distant from Port-Royal.

Vincent strongly urged the Missionaries to take vows,

which would stabilize them in the service to the poor. On October 19, 1641 he received approval to have the Missionaries make simple vows, while yet remaining within the secular clergy. The community's way of acting took shape during the retreats of 1632-35 (XI, 100). Father Portail jealously guarded the great letter of May 1, 1635 which detailed the religious and mystical basis of the apostolate. In July 1639 Saint Jeanne de Chantal received a compact description of the activity and spirit of the birth of the Company (I, 560).

The Daughters of Charity

The characteristics of the Daughters of Charity were still more quickly defined by Vincent. He gave them monthly conferences which, although we only have twelve from this period, reveal the vocation of these servants of the poor. They were called to love, serve and honor the human life of the Son of God, and they did this by praying, living in charity and mortifying themselves. In his January 1643 conference on the virtues of true Daughters of Charity, Vincent elaborated upon these fundamental directives (IX, 79-94).

His heartfelt concern was that this new group neither become a religious congregation (that would certainly have brought about its demise) nor relax in maintaining its unifying ideals of giving itself to God for the poor. The best way to achieve this was to keep them under the authority of the superior who had recruited them, namely, Vincent. The earliest statements of the Rules (1633, 1634, 1636) did not yet make this explicit, but it was always of capital importance to Louise.

The first of these servants of the poor lived at the house of Louise de Marillac in the rue de Versailles. Vincent then secured a house for them at La Chapelle and by 1641 they relocated to Saint Laurent very close to Saint Lazare. By 1643 there were nine houses which were open to the poor.

The Ladies of Charity

The increasingly complex and diverse nature of the Charities in the provinces and in Paris called for all Vincent's tact and diplomacy. He succeeded completely and the Hôtel-Dieu Confraternity, established in 1634 and presided over by Madame Goussault during its first five years, early on became the model for others. Madame Goussault recruited an initial group of 120 Ladies of Charity, soon joined by two hundred more who faithfully cared for the poor sick of this large hospital.

The Visitation Convent of Sainte-Marie

The fourth arena for Vincent's energies was the Visitation Convent of Saint Mary. During Mother Jane Frances de Chantal's visits to Paris in 1628, 1635 and 1641, Vincent often met with her, advised her and gave her spiritual direction. He also corresponded with her. His advice and counsel in the letters showed the clear influence of Francis de Sales. He found himself by God's gift mystically drawn into the spirit and fire of Saint Francis de Sales and Saint Jane de Chantal. When she died in Moulins, Vincent was supernaturally aware of it. As he celebrated Mass, he beheld a vision of her soul joining that of Francis de Sales and the two together being united to the Divine Essence (1641; XIII, 125-28).

Vincent did not share all of her views regarding the direction of the Visitation. He had, nevertheless, a profound personal regard for her and esteemed her with a religious reverence. It was of Jane de Chantal that Pierre de Bérulle said, "Her heart is an altar where the fire of love will never be extinguished but will consume the altar."

In devoting himself to her and to her daughters, he benefited from her spirit and her ardor. It was in her spirit and that of the Bishop of Geneva that Vincent consoled, exhorted and directed the Visitation Nuns of Saint Mary's. As time passed he came to be in charge of four monasteries.

Works on a National Scale

We can imagine that the administration and direction of these works was enough to occupy and fill one lifetime. But that's not what happened. Imperceptibly and without choosing it, Vincent entered into the life of the whole country. He entered into its heart while experiencing its traumas.

In 1636 the Imperial forces advanced on Paris and occupied Corbie. Saint-Lazare was transformed into a military camp and a distribution center for weapons. "The drum begins to beat as early as 7:00 a.m.," wrote Vincent, "and in the last eight days seventy-two companies arrived . . . the stable, the woodshed, the halls and cloister are filled with arms and the courtyard with soldiers" (I, 340). Chancellor Seguier asked for twenty Missionaries to serve as chaplains to the soldiers. Vincent was able to provide ten. He wrote a brief rule for them and accompanied them to Senlis. "Already four thousand soldiers have received the sacrament of Penance," wrote Vincent in September (I, 347).

One year later Vincent was impelled to take charge of a new and urgent work: the children who were abandoned (1638). Each year more than three hundred children were abandoned in the streets of Paris and the Saint-Landry shelter. "Many of them were sold for eight sous to beggars who would break their arms and legs or let them die of hunger" (XIII, 798). It was estimated that between 1600 and 1638 twelve thousand children died of hunger and neglect. In the beginning Vincent entrusted some of the children to Louise de Marillac. But, before long, embracing the entire work, he assigned a dozen Daughters of Charity to it and had thirteen houses built to receive the children. In 1647, he provided shelter at Bicêtre Castle and in 1649 he likewise used the hospice of the *Enfermés*.

At the beginning of 1639 Vincent undertook his first great crusade of charity. At the beginning of January, he became aware of the extreme distress of Lorraine, plundered by war, plague and famine. He appealed to the Ladies of Charity, and during the next ten years he did not stop sending help. His Missionaries' letters documented the number of tragic situations he responded to during that time:

- in Verdun, four to six hundred poor people, fifty to sixty sick people and thirty indigent persons were helped;
- in Metz, four to five thousand beggars were supported;
- in Pont-à-Mousson, five hundred beggars were fed;
- in Nancy, five hundred beggars and 180 very poor people were looked after. Toul did not send any news, but we know du Coudray gave of himself body and soul;
- in St-Mihiel, Father Guérin fed eleven hundred;
- in Bar-le-Duc, Fathers Montevit and Boucher assisted eight hundred hungry people on a permanent basis and nursed twenty-five sick people.

These centers of assistance were kept going by Brother Mathieu Regnard who, in disguise, crossed enemy lines undetected. He made fifty-three trips, each time transporting twenty-five to thirty thousand livres.

From Saint-Lazare, Vincent exhorted, consoled, advised and begged all to be patient. He organized missions for the refugees, received young women in danger, helped Mother Catherine de Bar and the Benedictines of Holy Sacrament Convent and mobilized assistance for the Lorraine nobility.

All these works brought Vincent into the limelight and people of prominence paid attention to him. Politicians sought his advice and invited him into their confidence. Richelieu, impressed with the Tuesday Conferences and retreats for ordinands, gave financial support to Vincent. He consulted him on the validity of the marriage of Gaston of Orleans to Marguerite de Lorraine.

The founder of the Mission took advantage of these meetings with ruling officials to plead for peace, and urged Richelieu to help the Irish people. Louis XIII, whose constant concern was the reform of the Church, obtained a list from Vincent of those whom he judged the most worthy of the episcopate. When he was dying, he called Vincent to assist him in his last agony. As soon as the Regency Council formed, Anne of Austria summoned Vincent to new responsibilities. Tempted to flee, Vincent decided to accept his public role. Where else could he be more useful to the poor?

International Activity (1643-60)

When Vincent de Paul took his place for the first time on the Council of Conscience in June 1643, he was in his sixty-third year. His activity found its own rhythm and became so extensive we can only paint the picture with broad strokes.

The Mission

Among his own confreres at Saint-Lazare, Vincent oversaw the works which had their origin at the motherhouse: the spiritual exercises for the ordinands and retreats for laity and clergy. The refectory fed two hundred people daily. Vincent wrote and updated the Rules for Missionaries and distributed them finally on May 17, 1658. Gradually he had persuaded his companions of the importance of taking vows. In 1655 the Holy See approved his formula and on January 25, 1656 most of his Missionaries renewed their commitments.

Vincent directed the Nuns of the Visitation, presided over their Council and sustained their spiritual life through conferences and letters.

He wrote or dictated on the average ten letters a day and starting in 1645 and 1646 enlisted the help of two secretaries, Brother Ducourneau and Brother Robineau.

Each week he gave the Missionaries a conference and held two repetitions of prayer.

The activity of the Congregation of the Mission extended beyond France to Italy (Genoa and Turin), Ireland and Scotland. To assist the slaves spiritually, priests and brothers of the Mission were placed on the consulate staffs of Tunis and

Algiers. A group of Missionaries left for Madagascar in 1648, and, in 1651, another for Poland. The Tuesday Conferences continued and grew to include Saintes, Marseilles, Ales, Turin, Le Puy, Angoulême, Angers, Bordeaux and Val Richer. Priests from the provinces wrote to Vincent for advice.

Daughters of Charity

The Daughters of Charity received a conference from Vincent each month. Records of one hundred and twenty of these have been preserved. Vincent followed the process and proceedings necessary to have their Constitutions approved patiently and with deep interest. On January 18, 1655 Jean François Paul de Gondi, the Archbishop of Paris, approved the fourth draft of the Constitutions, which then received civil approbation from the king and the parlement in 1657 and 1658.

Ladies of Charity

By 1647, as the misery deepened, the zeal of the Ladies of Charity was dwindling and their work with the foundling children was being endangered. Vincent summoned the women and addressed them with an appeal full of pathos, simplicity and humanity.

Ladies, your charity and compassion have led you to adopt these small creatures as your children. You have been their mothers by grace since their natural mothers have abandoned them. See now if you, too, can abandon them and, ceasing to be their mothers, become their judges. Their lives or deaths are in your hands. I am going to count your votes. It is time to pronounce sentence and know if you no longer wish to have mercy on them. These children will live if your love continues to care for them. On the contrary, they will die and certainly perish if you abandon them. Your experience will not let you doubt it. (XIII, 801)

The death sentence was not pronounced. The Ladies of Charity immediately agreed to remain protectors of the abandoned children.

The Great Emphases

All the above activities were built upon works that had been started earlier, so that in this phase of his life Vincent can be seen as a director of operations or chief executive officer. From 1643 onwards, however, Vincent became a minister of affairs in the larger sense of the word and, although he was without portfolio and officially had no cabinet level position, he had significant power in four arenas of France's life.

The Council of Conscience

The first arena was concern for the administration of public affairs and for public morality. He opposed visionaries, and had a close eye kept on new books and publications. He campaigned against duels and blasphemy. He closed the curtain on licentious comedies and scandalous processions. He was especially vigilant in seeing to the just conferral of benefices and the nomination of worthy candidates to the episcopacy. He joined with the Community of the Blessed Sacrament in founding hospitals, initiating visitation programs for prisoners and in sheltering displaced priests.

In 1642 he became vicar general of Richelieu-Vignerods and kept a vigilant eye on the regularity of the abbeys. His role here can be compared to a Secretary of State for Religious Affairs or to a Minister of the Interior, who was particularly concerned with administrative and public morality.

The Devastated Provinces

Secondly, Vincent was a minister to the devastated regions of France. He was unrelenting in his support of Lorraine from

1639 onwards and between 1650 and 1660 three other regions called for help.

At the first stirrings of the Parisian Fronde, Picardy and Champagne were methodically plundered, burned and devastated by the enemy. Vincent responded with an organized campaign of assistance. He then launched an information campaign based on his personal knowledge of the situation to encourage the people. About four thousand of these reports were printed and distributed monthly. The last of them dates from December 1655.

His campaign was reinforced first by a pastoral letter from the Archbishop of Paris. Then a well-known lawyer named Antoine Lemaitre published *Christian Alms* which expounded the ecclesial tradition regarding charity toward the poor. Next the future bishop of Venice, Antoine Godeau, published *Exhortation to the Parisians Regarding Alms*. These publications gave support to public preaching in favor of the poor.

The Ladies of Charity met weekly and according to their own method divided up their visits to the poor. With the aid of the Community of the Blessed Sacrament Vincent appointed an Administrator General of the Charities, first Father Berthe and then Father Alméras. It was their plan to receive in each locale the requests which priests, religious, Daughters of Charity and Confraternities of Charity relayed through the Missionaries.

The cries of the poor were many:

- at Guise and La Fère, 35 plundered villages, 600 destitute and 500 sick;
- at Laon, 100 plundered churches with priests and religious abandoned and destitute;
- at Soissons, 25 devastated churches in 30 villages and 1,200 sick;
- at Saint-Quentin, 7,000 to 8,000 poor, 1,200 refugees, 350 sick, 300 families left in poverty and 50 priests destitute;

- at Rheims, almost all churches plundered and the priests dispersed, killed or wounded.

His army of charity faced up to the soaring misery. The dead were buried, refugees, sick people, religious, orphans and young women were evacuated or hospitalized. A monthly salary was allocated to priests. Money, food, cloth and clothing were distributed. Economic and religious life was reorganized. Work tools, seed and religious objects were distributed. New Confraternities of Charity were founded. A total of five hundred thousand livres was spent between 1650 and 1660.

While the hands of the people were still held out to Vincent for help in Picardy and Champagne, the Ile-de-France was being engulfed by the miseries of sickness, murder and plunder. Consequently, in 1652 a third front was opened in Paris in spite of diminished resources. How, after all, could anyone remain insensitive to such distress?

At Port-Royal 240 religious were received, after having been expelled from their convents and abandoned to the streets. The number of beggars in Paris increased to more than one hundred thousand. In the Saint-Medard and Saint-Marcel districts nearly twenty-four thousand families were living in squalor. Every day about one hundred died at Hôtel-Dieu. More than ten thousand deaths were reported per month in Paris. The suburbs were a repugnant and lamentable spectacle.

Vincent was seventy-two at the time, but advanced age did not hamper him for a moment. At Saint-Lazare he provided soup twice each day for thousands of poor people. In June 1652, the Daughters of Charity fed eight hundred refugees at their motherhouse. In Saint Paul's parish, they fed five thousand poor people and nursed sixty to eighty patients.

Vincent assembled the abandoned ecclesiastics who roamed Paris. He rented a house for religious expelled from their convents and entrusted them to the Visitation Sisters. Women from the countryside received shelter, food and protection in a house in the Faubourg Saint-Denis.

Vincent refined and adjusted his charitable approaches. Not only did he seek to keep everyone informed, he organized collections. Wagons collected donations from butchers and clothiers. Every week, five to six thousand pounds of meat, two to three thousand eggs and provisions of clothing and utensils were sent to relieve needs of neighboring areas. The presbyteries served as the initial warehouses from which the gifts were then sent to the town-houses of respected women. They were shipped from there to the distribution centers.

Suburbs were divided into districts and assigned to religious communities such as the Jesuits, Augustinians, Carmelites, Capuchins and Picpus Fathers who monitored the spiritual and material needs of the people. Vincent's Missionaries had special charge over two suburbs. Work and sickness decimated them, but volunteers immediately took their place. The work went on. In Etrechy, Villeseneux and Saint-Arnoult soup kitchens opened and about thirty villages were helped.

Doctrinal Disputes

The third arena concerned faith and doctrine, in which Vincent was called upon to act with speed and energy. He seems to have taken a position against the Jansenists as early as 1641. As a member of the Council of Conscience he could show no equivocation. Rome had condemned the Jansenist doctrine in *In Eminenti*, and Vincent in 1649 gathered a group of bishops at Saint-Lazare to put an end to discussions. He gave his encouragement to the head of the faculty of the University of Paris, who had summarized the Five Propositions of *Augustinus*. He campaigned among the bishops to obtain their commitment and was able to gather eighty-eight signatures. He personally went to Port-Royal and met with the solitaries to make their submission easier.

In spite of his successful efforts in bringing calm to the situation, the results were mixed. He was resented for his opposition to Antoine Arnauld. Vincent had condemned Arnauld's excessively rigoristic pastoral letter both in public and at the Council of Conscience, when it was learned that Easter communions were down substantially at Saint Sulpice (down three thousand) and Saint-Nicolas-du-Chardonnet (down fifteen hundred). In 1655-56 the conflict between Picote and the Duke of Liancourt exhausted Vincent's power as mediator. Before he was able to work out a reconciliation, the *Pétites lettres* of Pascal moved the debate into the public forum. Port-Royal had the last laugh; there was nothing more to do.

Politics

In the world of politics, Vincent's attitude was significantly more complex. He found himself precariously poised between the need to remain neutral in quarrels among Christian leaders and the need to take a stand when the well-being of his flock demanded it. How, in the midst of the melee between the Fronde and the Regency, could he at the same time do what was right, continue sympathy and recognition of Cardinal de Retz and oppose Mazarin's actions? Mazarin, though he sided with Vincent to neutralize the influence of Port-Royal and protect the sovereignty of Anne of Austria and the young Louis XIV, could not forgive Vincent his influence upon the queen. His notebooks document his bitter resentment.

Their antagonism burst into the open when, on January 6, 1649, Vincent asked Mazarin to resign. Anne of Austria denied his request and Vincent wandered the roads of France for the next six months. He only returned to Paris when the Court did.

Despite Vincent's prudent efforts, the struggle had become public. Vincent's full support of Cardinal de Retz became apparent in 1654-55. Mazarin had the impetuous archbishop imprisoned at Vincennes and then at Nantes. He escaped and took refuge in the house of the Mission in Rome. Mazarin was furious and got Louis XIV to close the house in Rome. Vincent announced the event to his Missionaries and asked them to thank God for the grace which had permitted his Company to exercise both obedience to the king and fidelity to their friends.

Anne of Austria, who chose to remain at the periphery of these conflicts, always kept Vincent in high regard. She knew of all that he did for the poor and how he had helped save Lorraine and the foundlings. One day in an outburst of generosity she personally placed in his hands jewels worth eighteen thousand livres. Nonetheless, her personal preferences and her ties to Mazarin considerably limited Vincent's influence. Though he had some success in politics, his true mission was elsewhere.

A Balance Sheet

In keeping with his dreams and his prayer, Vincent did not die in bed. He died in battle, fully armed, fighting for the poor. Since that day in 1617 when he sided with the poor, he had spent forty-three years fighting against sin, misery, fatigue and sickness. The latter in July 1660 confined him to his room. In spite of this, he struggled and worked on. When his pain abated, sleep overcame and exhausted him. "It is the brother who waits for his sister to come," he would say. Death literally made him light up. A witness tells us, "At the moment of his death, he surrendered his beautiful soul into the hands of the Lord and, seated there, he was handsome, more majestic and venerable to look at than ever" (XIII, 191).

It was September 27, 1660, at the hour for prayer. The dawn was gently breaking.

In the great void which he left behind, he appeared to his followers as before — astonishingly rich and complex in his giftedness. He had the physique of a peasant, not tall, perhaps five feet four inches, solidly built of sand and stone, but he had labored like a giant.

An account of his works might read as follows. Between 1628 and 1660, thirteen or fourteen thousand ordinands attended the ordination retreats. The house of Saint-Lazare alone gave more than one thousand missions. Twenty thousand retreatants were housed at Saint-Lazare and the College des Bons-Enfants. Almost ten thousand children were rescued from certain death. Hundreds of thousands of poor people were helped.

The moral balance sheet goes beyond numbers. A new idea was taking shape during his lifetime. Vincent himself introduced a new form of religious life. He was one of the most able and perhaps the best of the reformers of the clergy. His innovations reached beyond the religious whom he encouraged and the episcopate he purified. More than anyone, Vincent had restored good taste and simplicity to preaching, and in a word, the feeling and power of the gospel.

If all his works were to vanish and all his achievements come to naught, Vincent himself would remain an inexhaustible wellspring of spiritual inspiration and strength. Thanks to him over the course of a number of years, God's invisible friendship had become visible and radiant in the hearts and bodies of people.

His Spiritual Way

Introduction

Surprise

Vincent would have been surprised to hear anyone speak of his spiritual doctrine. Except for the small booklet, *The Common Rules or Constitutions of the Congregation of the Mission*, he was reluctant to publish his ideas and convictions. Even these Rules were not the result of his own individual effort according to his way of thinking, for they had evolved from the experience of his religious community. Like most founders, he wanted only to offer his Missionaries a summary of the gospels and point out to them a quick, simple and sure way to live them.

Pascal wrote, "We were expecting to find an author, and we found a man." Vincent had done all within his power not to be treated as an author. He only allowed Mademoiselle Legras to keep notes on his conferences for the benefit of those who were absent. He did, however, often help her edit and summarize them (III, 23; II, 358 - January 25, 1643; August 25, 1646).

His attitude toward his Missionaries was very different. He would have been angry had he known that some of his conferences were being recorded by them. Fortunately, no one was foolish enough to ask his permission or to let him know it was being done. As soon as a conference was over, some of the confreres present summarized what Vincent had said. Three years before his death, that is in 1657, Fathers Alméras and Dehorgny officially but secretly commissioned Brother Bertrand Ducournau to do this work. The collection

48

of conferences thus preserved has been estimated as no more than one-fortieth of those Vincent delivered to his Missionaries between 1625 and 1660.

In view of these facts, the question has sometimes been asked whether it is possible to discern clearly the substance of his thought, its organization and originality. Even among his own, there are those who hesitate to answer yes unequivocally.

Uncertainties

Guillaume Delville published a brief sketch of the Congregation of the Mission in 1656, in which he named obedience rather than mortification as one of the Congregation's fundamental virtues.

Brother Ducournau said Vincent was different with different audiences. Vincent "ordinarily spoke only of commonplace topics to spiritual and learned persons, though he spoke of them with uncommon energy and power. When Vincent spoke [however] of the virtues proper to Missionaries, he waxed eloquent concerning both their practice and their expression" (see XII, 447).

In this light we can understand how Abelly, Vincent's first biographer, changed his mind. He declared in the first edition (1664) that the imitation of the Lord was Vincent's principal virtue (Abelly, L. I., p. 78). Later in 1667, he defined Vincent's spirit through two essential virtues: the imitation of the Lord and conformity to God's will. It was this edition which Vincentian readers accepted as the classical text between 1667 and 1748. In 1748, Collet in his *Life of Saint Vincent de Paul* revived the 1664 notion of a single virtue and this assertion was not afterwards contradicted. The re-editions of Abelly from then to the present day have been made from the 1664 edition, and leave the impression that the imitation of Christ is the sole identifying characteristic of Vincent's life.

Problems Facing Vincent's Biographers

The conviction that Vincent's spirituality was adequately explained in his imitation of the Lord lasted well into the twentieth century. As a result, biographers concentrated on the events of Vincent's life and simply treated his spirituality thematically. Only now are we in a position to fully delve into Vincent's interiority.

Biographers have taken two approaches to reveal Vincent's secret. The first approach focused on Vincent's prodigious activity, which was astonishing by any set of standards. Abelly followed this way. The chronology of religious and political events alone was a challenge. Vincent's activities were local, regional, national, international, spiritual, ecclesiastical, political, charitable and societal. Little happened in France that he did not know about and to which he did not respond, to the degree possible. In this sea of activity, it was easy to lose sight of Vincent's personal journey and the mystery of his interior life. The biographers following Abelly likewise were unable to escape the magnetic field of Vincent's ceaseless energy. Vincent's activity continued to overshadow his interiority.

Vincent's biographers were aware of this dilemma, but believed the spiritual and edifying side of Vincent's life could be handled in a book on his virtues, following the outline of the three theological virtues and four moral virtues. Though these excerpts were without a context, either psychological, chronological or developmental, they did succeed in providing food for reflection and prayer.

The second approach started from the letters and conferences of Vincent, which were first published for the general public in 1881. The definitive edition of letters, conferences and documents by Pierre Coste in 1920-1925 set off a new wave of research, writing and reflection. The 8,000 pages of Coste's collection presented the challenge of how to faithfully present a synthesis of Vincent's work.

The letters, about four thousand of them, represented only one-eighth of Vincent's correspondence. They ranged from simple thank-you notes to circulars, orders and appointments. It was impossible to ignore Vincent's multiple occupations in them, yet it remained difficult to name with confidence his master ideas and his chief concerns. As a result of the uneven distribution of his writings over the various phases of his life, it was hard to follow the evolution and development of his spiritual life. From the period 1607 to 1624 only three isolated letters have survived. The conferences to the Missionaries from 1625 until 1645 were summarized in one hundred fifty pages. The conferences to the Daughters of Charity, representing twelve years of monthly talks (1633-45), were gathered in 280 pages. For the most part, his letters and conferences shed light only upon the last five years of his life (1655-60), thus they are the words of an old man speaking to us in his seventy-fifth to his eightieth years.

These difficulties explain why subsequent generations of Vincentians, who ventured to dig through the letters and conferences, had to follow some way to arrange and classify the texts. Some presented an anthology of writings, prayers, reflections and exhortations. This arrangement appealed to readers and had a market. Others organized the texts around Vincent's roles as priest, spiritual director and minister to the sick. This thematic arrangement of texts lacked a relationship to the events and activities of Vincent's life. Nevertheless, these sayings were both inspiring and beneficial to their readers.

Some writers trained in spirituality or sociology attempted to make Vincent a disciple in the school of a spiritual master by studying the influence of others upon him. In that light his associations with Bérulle, Francis de Sales and Ignatius Loyola were carefully examined. These studies did not succeed because Vincent's genius and originality put him beyond such reductive classification.

A Doctrine in a Life

Vincent was versatile, prolific and humble to such a degree that he eludes all schemes of simplifying his life and classifying him. A person had to be around him for only a short while to be convinced he was not a speculative person. He had none of the doctrinal originality of a Bérulle, an Olier, a Condren. On the other hand, whatever his attitude was when he quoted Bérulle, imitated Francis de Sales and made their images and thoughts his own, he always remained an independent person. He wasn't their disciple in the usual academic meaning of this word. He did not mechanically adopt what they said as a master's principles and directives or confine himself to a single director or school. He was open and welcomed all of them. When he turned to favorite masters such as Bérulle, Francis de Sales, Rodriquez, Vincent Ferrier, Benet of Canfield or Duval, he always took what they provided with respect but maintained his complete independence. While adopting their offerings, he adapted them and often transformed them. His originality was not in matters of doctrine, but *in life and in experience*. His recommendations emerged not from scholastic deduction but from practical experience.

Our best chance of grasping the shape of his originality comes from the three areas in which he felt most at ease and was considered a master by his contemporaries: experience, faith and practical wisdom.

Experience

Vincent claimed that he was quite ignorant and insisted he never got very far in school. This admission delighted Saint-Cyran, Lancelot, Dom Gerberon and those Jansenists who, seeking to discredit him, accused him of being ignorant and intellectually narrow. Vincent was not phased by it in the least.

He knew that great ideas, tightly reasoned arguments,

beautiful thoughts at prayer and finely turned phrases in preaching had only a relative value. He was sensitive to practical matters and at one time was attracted by the empirical sciences of alchemy and medicine. He thought monuments of syllogistic reasoning and complex theories which did nothing to improve human lives were unreal. Yet, he wasn't lacking in finesse. He was one of those who, according to Pascal, "judge from the heart, because they choose to approach things from the point of view of values, and are not accustomed to look for the principles involved." (quoted from Brunschvicg, minor, 3) Vincent affirmed this in his own words: "We believe a person, not because he is well informed, but because we consider him good and we love him. Our Savior himself let his love be known to those whom he wanted to have faith in him."

Vincent's ideas cannot be isolated and reduced to abstract propositions. They were inspired and protected by love, which animated them, and expressed the life which bore and nurtured them. Love for Vincent was not a consequence of his thought. On the contrary, his thought was, like a daughter, the expression of his love. His life was experience, and his experience carried and confirmed his doctrine. This explains the radical source of dynamism in his life. He did not pass from ideas to action or to a way of living, as if he had made a firm resolution at an inspiring retreat. Everything leads us to believe that even after his contacts with Monsieur de Bérulle and Monsieur Duval, his intellectual achievements did not attract much attention.

From 1613 to 1617, as his significant experiences opened up to a deliberate pattern of life, Vincent clearly began to formulate what he had begun to live. He paid close attention to events and even closer attention to the people who gave meaning to the events. As he was being purified by grace and trials, he tried to decipher their meaning and made a response. When he discovered it was his mission to remedy the ignorance of the poor and the priests, he sought ways to respond.

The rhythm and steps of his way are revealed in these favorite words of his: "It's necessary to give oneself to God (*se donner*) . . . in order to serve the poor . . . to go on Mission . . . to direct seminaries and ordinands. . . ." When this gift had been made, Vincent was immediately able to take from everyone who came his way (Francis de Sales, Pierre de Bérulle, Saint Thérèse, Saint Ignatius, André Duval, Benet of Canfield), the word or practice or disposition which fitted the situation and helped the most. The worth of each human being is in the action which gives truth to his or her existence. Such action for him consisted in rendering Christ present and letting him act in oneself, in making oneself present to Christ and in acting for him. In his name, *In Nomine Domini . . . In the name of Our Lord Jesus Christ.*

Begin with action. Vincent used to take pleasure in emphasizing each word from the gospels. " 'Seek' is only a word," he said, "but I think it tells us much. It means to have the disposition of desiring always to do what is recommended to us, to work untiringly for the kingdom of God, not to let ourselves be unoccupied or idle, to pay attention to our interior life and regulate it and not pay attention to the exterior life and its amusements. *Seek, seek* means *care*, it means action" (XII, 131). Vincent's definition of love and zeal is well known: "If the love of God is fire, zeal is its flame" (XII, 307-08).

Vincent often came back to the first chapter of the Acts of the Apostles, where the life of Jesus is summarized by Luke in terms of "all that Jesus did and taught." On the basis of this expression, Vincent proclaimed the radical priority of action. If being comes before doing, so, living the truth comes before teaching it. "We must begin by establishing the kingdom of God in ourselves and only then in others" (cf. II, 97). "It's necessary to tend to our interior life. If we fail to do that, we miss everything" (XII, 131).

Action in this sense was not merely an expenditure of physical energy or something instinctively satisfying. For Vin-

cent it was the main and perhaps the only way to unite oneself
to invisible reality, to God's will and to God himself. "We have
to sanctify our occupations, by seeking God in them and by
doing them to find God in them rather than to get them done."
(XII, 132) Only this intention of going beyond the visible in
our actions gives value to action.

As we pay attention to the *goal* action has in view, we see
it is not a lifeless ideal. It is a living and loving person, the
Christ. "Nothing pleases me," Vincent affirmed, "but in Jesus
Christ" (Abelly, I, 78).

An invisible person is the magnetic pole which orients
Vincent's profound thoughts, his preferences, his way of
speaking. His talks are full of aphorisms and quotations, but
he never uses them as absolute principles or constraints on
his thought. They are brush strokes and embellishments to
invoke a Life. Even the evangelical maxims are nothing other
than condensations of the life of Christ. They have no intrinsic
power of their own, they are only the expressions of the
power of Jesus, who expresses himself through them and *in*
them. "Our Lord—not evangelical quotations—is the rule of the
Mission." (XII, 130)

Faith

Reality in the Invisible and in Christ

What is visible is not the only reality. Nor is it the deepest
reality, only its shadow. We may be surprised at all the
changes and variations on life's theme, yet the scriptures tell
us that we ourselves do not remain in the same state. Change
and variation reveal a deeper reality. Anyone who is unaware
of the fragile and tenuous nature of what is created will build
on shifting sands. The wise person, however, builds upon
rock, which no one can attack and cannot be shaken. Experience proves that "only eternal truths can satisfy our hearts."
(Abelly, III, 9)

Vincent did not stop at abstract archetypes and eternal essences. Rather he built upon the teachings and promises of the gospel. This Eternal Foundation is actually a life, which, we might say, came to expression in the face of Christ.

The Christ whom Vincent contemplated and adored is not a representation of an eternal truth, but a living human being united with humankind in history, on a mission from his Father to save humanity. It was the Father's love which involved him in this mission that consisted in the self-emptying of the incarnation and of his sufferings and his death. The missionary Christ is at the heart of the redemptive movement, and it is in this movement we have to place ourselves. Every person is called to associate himself or herself with the mysterious adventure of the incarnate Word.

Rapidly and with a firm hand Vincent paints for us a portrait of the interiority of Jesus. Coming from the Father's side, the Son of God is immersed in unconditional esteem, honor, love. This "experience" leads him to give himself (*se donner*). It likewise puts him in radical opposition to the world of evil, which, according to Saint John, is the concupiscence of the eyes, the concupiscence of the flesh and the pride of life.

The Achievement of Christ

Christ lives on after his death in the Church, which is his living presence in every time and place and the living expression of his Spirit. We might call it the home of Jesus. If this is so, then, just as Jesus addressed himself to the poor, and just as he lived as a poor person, and just as he is represented to us by the poor, so the Church of Jesus is centered on the poor and has to organize itself around them. Like Jesus, the Church, animated by the Spirit of God, must address itself first of all to the poor, who in the eyes of faith are the privileged assistants of God. It is they who open to us the gates of eternity. When we have the faith "to turn the medal over," as Saint Vincent said, we will see in poor people the living image of the life and death of Jesus.

They have a mysterious effect upon us. By their presence, they ask us to adapt to them. In taking Christ's attitude toward them, we find dispositions growing in ourselves which lead to evangelization, especially, to a love that is open to the faces of poverty and humility.

In this way the life of Jesus begins to take hold in human hearts. This life, which has been merited by the death of Jesus, does not take effect, to tell the truth, automatically. It requires human acceptance. To live in Christ Jesus, we have to consent to die in Christ Jesus. It is the mystical death initiated through baptism. It is a life of dying, a life like that of Christ on earth. We die in Jesus Christ paradoxically through the life of Jesus Christ.

Without doubt, this life in and through Christ remains hidden and mysterious. It asks for everything, for death to self. Without the detachment and humility which empties us of self, we cannot *truly* live in Christ nor can Christ act in us. It's in persons empty of self that Christ not only dwells, but acts and bears fruit. Jesus, the Christ, is the unique source of all our life and action.

Practical Wisdom

"Monsieur Vincent's character," Father de Condren once said, "is marked by practical wisdom" ("prudence" in French). It consisted very precisely of making his life conform to the way incarnate Wisdom had lived and spoken. For him practical wisdom, simplicity and purity of intention were all one reality.

What was his way of letting eternal Wisdom guide him? Vincent appealed most often to three precepts which gave a distinctive character to his life in Christ and in God.

The first precept has to do with *purity of intention and singleness of purpose*. Vincent often repeated, "It is necessary to begin with God, to look to God first, to ask for a share in God's Spirit and a share in God's view of things" (XII, 139).

"It is necessary to begin with the things of God. When we take care of God's business, God will take care of ours" (cf. XII, 139). "It is necessary to see things as they are in God, and not as they appear, otherwise we will err gravely" (cf. VII, 388).

The second precept expresses and regulates our *rootedness in the invisible*. When do we know whether the actions which give us to God grasp us totally? The answer is: when they effectively embrace "the extremes." Affective love must always be coupled with effective love, otherwise, it is an illusion. Likewise, inner mortification must always be matched by outer mortification, otherwise, "one gives evidence of being mortified neither interiorly nor exteriorly" (cf. XI, 71). Even the love of God and union with God must take account of another term. "It is not enough for me to love God," Vincent proclaimed, "if my neighbor does not love God" (XII, 262). Union with our neighbor is necessary for union with God.

The final precept deals with *rules for action*. Just as God's actions are rooted within his unchangeable divine essence and his purposes are unchangeable and eternal, the goal of human action must likewise be firm and unwavering. But God also varies his expression and ways of reaching us, now embracing us, now withdrawing, appearing to progress in time by using changing events. We have to use time and events, consequently, to adapt ourselves more deeply to God and literally be in communion with what God does and does not will (God's will and non-will).

For Vincent, then, the heart and soul of genuine action was to be "firm and invariable concerning the goal, gentle and flexible concerning the means" (cf. II, 335).

These three precepts give to the so-called "doctrine" of Vincent its shape and characteristic features:
- Life must expand constantly through action.
- Life and action receive their depth and truth only through faith.
- Life lived in faith must grow and adapt, in order to remain faithful to the goal of eternal life.

The Daughters of Charity and his missionaries experienced in Vincent the personification of this practical wisdom. Vincent in his turn outlined what was to be done through the virtues suited to the vocation and state of each community. He asked the missionaries to practice five virtues (simplicity, humility, meekness, mortification and zeal). The Daughters were taught to adhere to three (humility, simplicity and charity). Each of his sons and daughters, in looking to Vincent, had a clear picture of who to be and what to do as Jesus' followers.

People regularly said Vincent never changed. "Monsieur Vincent is always Monsieur Vincent." He is the unchanging tenderness of God. At the same time everyone thought of him as extremely flexible and adaptable. Paradoxically, this intuitive man, whose feelings and impulsive nature left unchecked had a potential for disaster, impressed his listeners as reserved and radiated a peacefulness many thought miraculous. He had a gift for presenting his thoughts and sentiments concretely and clearly. He moved effortlessly from reflections to stories about daily life, gracefully weaving the visible and invisible together. His Gasconian finesse was an ally to his naturally respectful and affectionate ways. More than just calling Jesus to mind, Vincent through his words, introduced Jesus to people and put them in the presence of his mystery among the poor.

The Spirit and Mystery of Charity

These three precepts taken alone, however, would risk missing the best part of Vincent's spirit. If we had had the opportunity to watch Vincent addressing his Missionaries or the Daughters of Charity or unlearned folks or the spiritually advanced, we would have noticed that his words were nothing more than a vehicle for his transcendent spirit, a "sign." His words were like clothing to his spirit, meant to protect and express it. If we were to stop at his words and reduce them to an organized and edifying "spiritual doctrine," the life would go from them and they would lose their power to nourish our spirits, give heart to our works and lead us to God. We would be caught in what might be regarded as Vincentian fundamentalism.

Famous for his passion to catechize, Vincent — the peasant become saint — had a still greater gift. He could transmit his conviction that doctrine was the effort of one life to assist the blossoming of another life: the life of Jesus in human hearts. It was not a collection of concepts or series of principles. The value of teaching for him, then, was found in what it led to and what it called forth.

Smiling gently, Vincent discouraged every consecration of formulas and canonization of methods. He loved order, rigor, method and precision, but avoided reducing them to arithmetic formulas. His spirit came through the words. He led people irresistibly beyond dwelling on words and phrases to coming face to face with the essential task: emptying oneself of self and offering oneself to the Christ who gives himself to souls. "It is necessary to empty oneself of self in order to be filled with God, it is necessary to give oneself to God in order to be emptied of self." Sometimes he reversed the formula, but it didn't matter. It's easy to see and feel what's essential: to give oneself (*se donner*).

He exercised the same liberty regarding words when he renewed their spiritual meaning. For example, religious uniformity. He reminded everyone of its value and how continuity was opposed to nature's instincts and constrained us to be reasonable. But he knew sclerosis, inflexibility and rigidity were equally fatal illnesses of the soul. The one who repeats the same thing over and over again changes more than one might suppose. But the change is for the worse. The secret of continuity is in fidelity. God, working unceasingly, unceasingly invites us to associate ourselves with his initiatives, to support his gracious ingenuity and to reveal the remarkable forms of his unique love.

Vincent said also, "Let us be committed and keep our hands to the plow." Yet, it would be a mistake to interpret this saying rigidly. True commitment is firm but thoroughly flexible. It is full of vital energy. It becomes strong and rich by its open desire for communion with all things, and by its determination to let the sunlight of divine kindness melt the steel-plated armor of self-love.

It's with this kind of humble tenacity that Vincent conducted his novitiate of charity. His most virtuous followers knew they would only become fully professed in eternity. Both alternating bouts of weakness and energetic fervor and the doubts which cloud our first certainties cast a shadow over our efforts to become fully mature apostles of charity.

The poor alone have some power over these abiding obstacles. Yet, we must be careful. No one has the right to use the poor as a means to another end. This would be a sacrilege. Even for the best of intentions we cannot colonize the poor in the name of "charity." This would be an invalidly baptized form of paternalism. It's lure would be as repugnant as that form of sentimental egoism which uses the sufferings of others as an outlet for personal pity.

The poor of God, whom Vincent loved, disturb our consciences rather than guarantee us good ones. The poor person does not forget God, for the reason that he or she cannot live without God. Poor men and women derive their power and nobility from the humiliated Christ, who has only their voice to make himself well understood. The eternal vocation of the poor is this: to denounce sensuality and self-love wherever it exists. Their power is immense, their insights acute. In the Church, they are the rich ones, the lords. Wherever they go, they light a fire which does not go out. In spite of their rags, they nurture all who live to serve them. Vincent became one of their most devoted servants. To all who, hungering for God, surrounded Vincent and asked for a "doctrine," he silently offered them the bread of the poor.

Tradition and Inspiration

In his armchair by the fire, Vincent fell asleep in the Lord, September 27, 1660. On that day he began a new career. His spirit was not able to remain at rest. He continued to be active in the institutions he founded, the spiritual direction he continues to give and the movements of spirit and heart he animates till the present day.

The Institutional Tradition

René Alméras became Vincent's successor in 1661. By that time the organization of the two religious families was practically complete. The superiors of both the Mission and the Daughters of Charity were devoted to their founder to such a degree that they felt it sacrilegious to make even the smallest change in the practices envisioned by such a holy teacher. Their main concerns were to sustain devotion to Vincent, record his life story and, above all, to maintain the institutions in the spirit he had given them.

The Expansion of Works (1660-1960)

This same view of things was common to all the superiors general until the time of the French Revolution, as they guided the works of charity emanating from Saint-Lazare. Two Generals in particular, M.E. Jolly and Jean Bonnet, made a deep impact upon the lives of both religious families.

The first, Father Jolly, whom Vincent indicated to the Duchess of Aiguillon as his successor, held the destiny of

Vincent's works in his hands for twenty-four years. He had a domineering character, which enabled him to withstand Louis XIV and Louvois. Between 1673 and 1697, he totally transformed the house of Saint-Lazare and opened forty new houses. The second, Jean Bonnet (1711-35), a conscientious administrator and vigilant pastor, took a clear stand against existing forms of Jansenism and was not afraid to dismiss about twenty confreres during his time. He also presided over the celebrations of Vincent's beatification in 1729, for which Father Pierron (1736-43) had done the spadework in Paris and Rome. But it was during the time of Father Couty, the seventh superior general (1736-43), that the canonization of Vincent by Pope Clement XII took place in 1737.

Without fanfare or interruption the Missionaries and Daughters of Charity quietly continued the works created by Vincent. The work of the seminaries developed considerably. By 1789, the Congregation of the Mission had fifty-five diocesan seminaries under its direction. The superior generals, however, bowing to the authority of the crown, consented to undertake works they judged to have little to do with the initial scope of the Company. It was thus that, in 1661, under the sway of Anne of Austria, the Vincentians accepted the royal parish at Fontaine-bleau. In 1674, they began to minister at the royal parish of Notre Dame of Versailles and, due to this title, became chaplains to the court. Parishioners and courtiers long remembered François Hevert (1651-1730) as "one of the most long-winded preachers of the kingdom." His known works include, in addition to the four volumes which he published, sixty volumes of sermons in Latin. He remained as the king's chaplain for twenty years. Louis XIV rewarded his zeal by appointing him Bishop of Agen. Father Vincent would not have been happy. It was likewise by the order of the king, that "the Goatees" (a nickname for the Vincentians) became chaplains at l'Hôtel des Invalides (1674) and the royal palace of Saint-Cyr (1690). They were obliged also to accept the parish of Saint-Louis-des-Invalides (1727) and the hospital of Saint-Cloud (1688).

Beyond French Borders

Many houses were opened throughout Europe. In Italy, seventeen houses were established between 1669 and 1734; in Poland, Russia and Polish Prussia, another seventeen between 1677 and 1719; and in 1704, the Spanish Mission began in Barcelona. The Missionaries were welcomed in Lisbon in 1734, Hungary in 1732, and in Heidelberg in 1781.

For 130 years the Mission's attentions were to European needs. Up until the Revolution, there were only three areas outside Europe where the missionary zeal of the Congregation was engaged: in Tunis and North Africa, in Madagascar (from 1648 to 1674) and in China. In 1712 Missionaries emigrated from Madagascar to Bourbon Island and in 1722 to Maurice Island. In China, the heroic efforts of Appiani, Mullener and Pedrini had failed, and by 1746 all had departed.

In 1791, the Congregation was made up of 168 houses; 55 French seminaries, most of which were affiliated with a parish or mission house; 990 members, of whom 508 were priests, 262 were brothers and nearly 200 were seminarians.

Daughters of Charity

The Daughters of Charity enjoyed a similar period of vigorous growth. In 1668, at the time Cardinal de Vendome, Legate of the Holy See, approved the Constitutions of the Daughters of Charity for a second time, the Daughters were established in 60 places. A half century later the Daughters were in 300 houses. By 1790 there were 450 houses, 20 of which were in Poland, and 120 novices at the motherhouse in Paris with a total of 4,300 sisters in the houses of Charity.

The French Revolution and the troubles which followed caused great torment for both religious families. If the Motherhouse of the Daughters of Charity was spared, the priory of Saint-Lazare was not. It was sacked on the eve of the Revolution, July 13, 1789. In 1792 at the Seminary of Saint-Firman, the old College des Bons-Enfants, the insurgents massacred the Missionaries and hurled their bodies out the windows. Sisters were executed in Arras, Angers, Mayenne and Dax. When the troubles were over, they needed years to take up their ordinary activities again.

The Saint-Laurent house, which was the Motherhouse, was reduced to rubble and the sisters relocated to a house in the Rue du Vieux-Colombier, which today is a fire station. It is there that His Holiness Pius VII came to them to bless them on December 23, 1804 and that they once again began to wear the "habit," and it is there that they renewed their vows at a Mass celebrated by Cardinal Fesch, on March 25, 1805. Thanks to an astonishing number of new members (there were 283 houses in 1806), they took up residence on June 28, 1815 at the Hotel Chatillon in the rue du Bac (the present 140 rue du Bac).

The Mission

The afflictions which the Mission suffered had been particularly cruel. The superior general was forced to flee from Saint-Lazare. He died in Rome on February 12, 1800. He was succeeded by Father Brunet, the Vicar General, and later by Father Hanon. But the quarrels which erupted between the latter and Napoleon I, who wanted to entrust the direction of the Daughters of Charity to the bishops, delayed the reorganization of the Mission considerably. The Convention suppressed the Company in 1792, but it was reestablished by Napoleon's decree of May 27, 1804. It survived until 1809 when it was again suppressed and Monsieur Hanon was thrown into prison. The Company had to wait until the fall of Napoleon, before it could again take up its legal status on February 3, 1816. A year later, on November 9, 1817, the Missionaries took up residence at the Hôtel de Lorges at 95 rue de Sèvres. It is in the chapel which they built there in 1826 that the relics of Saint Vincent were solemnly received on April 24, 1830. His relics had lost their resting place in 1792.

The loss of personnel during this time was no less considerable. Of the 508 priests who made up the personnel of the Congregation in France in 1792, there were scarcely one hundred at the disposition of the superior general in 1809.

Renaissance

Three superiors general, J.B. Etienne (who was called the second founder), Eugene Boré, and Antoine Fiat, were the artisans of the Congregation's renaissance in the nineteenth century. Under their leadership, the Congregation not only resumed its old functions, but acquired a missionary outlook which became one of its distinguishing characteristics.

When Clement XIV dissolved the Jesuits, the Vincentians took their place in China, as they were able. In the Near East they opened houses at Constantinople, Smyrna, Naxos, Thera, Salonica, Damascus, Alep, Tripoli and Antoura.

They entered the United States (1815), Brazil (1818), Ethiopia (1839), Iran (1841), Egypt and Mexico (1844), Chile (1853), Peru (1858), The Republic of Argentina (1859), Guatemala and the Philippines (1862), the Antilles (1863), Ecuador (1870), Columbia, Panama and Costa Rica (1877), Paraguay (1880), Uruguay (1884), Australia (1885), San Salvador (1898) and, in 1900, Palestine. On January 28, 1896, the Holy See entrusted the southern part of Madagascar to them.

During the twentieth century they entered Bolivia (1905), the Republic of Honduras (1910), the British Isles (1921), Java (1923), the Belgian Congo (1925), Canada (1955) and Vietnam (1956). In spite of legal restrictions, two world wars and Marxist persecutions, as of 1990 the Congregation of the Mission included 3,280 priests, 131 students, 4 permanent deacons, 252 Brothers and 516 admitted members (i.e., in some stage of formation). There are, in all, 4,214 members of which 31 are bishops.

As of 1960, the Company of the Daughters of Charity had 4,211 establishments and approximately 45,000 members.

They made up five percent of the number of religious worldwide. In 1990, there were approximately 32,000 Daughters.

The Two Expressions of the Vincentian Spirit

Let us step back for a moment. The three centuries in the history of charity, sustained over time by the same inspiration, have given birth, however, to two psychological types, two different ways of living the same grace. These two types reveal two ways of continuing the work of Vincent and being profoundly and totally faithful to him.

The Missionary Type

The first way refers to men and women whom people easily recognize as missionaries. They display a spirit of initiative and adventure and a taste for risk and capacity for adaptation. Whatever their country of origin, these Vincentians, who are rich in concern for others, are instinctively drawn to arduous work and difficult challenges. They have solid temperaments and are often known for original achievements, though they mask their innovative ways with a genial smile and a disarming expression of deep-seated modesty.

In this group which is wary of its power but unaware of its originality, we find the great missionary bishops of China and Ethiopia — pioneers such as Monsieurs Appiani and Mullener, Fathers Huc and Gabet, Saint Justin de Jacobis and Blessed Ghebré Michaël. Closer to our times, among the Lazarists of extraordinary stature, are Joseph Baetmann, Lobry, Sarloutte and Coulbeaux. If these zealous missionaries needed patrons or protectors, they might have selected Blessed Jean-Gabriel Perboyre (martyred in China in 1840) or Blessed Francis-Regis Clet. They scarcely had to think consciously of them, however, for they felt their presence in their lives. They will always have admirers, and, though few found biographers, it will have been enough for the Church that they lived.

The Contemplative Type

Less visible and less enchanting is the profile of the other psychological type in the Vincentian tradition. The ones who comprise this company align themselves with Chartreux, whose silence they honor. They find themselves in the company of teachers, who spend their lives in the routine of daily discipline. They are gathered in major and minor seminaries where they live out their commitment and bring their values to life. Their risks are taken silently and their adventures occur within the four walls of their studies or their classrooms.

Their outward appearance is modest. They are repelled and bored by worldly pursuits for they know their grace is elsewhere. Nourished by work and educated in simplicity, they dream of being true friends of humble and poor people. Their vocation? To welcome, to be a source of peace, to renounce self and live in that simplicity which facilitates the communion of hearts.

Do they need ancestors? They might find one in Du Coudray, who wanted to translate the Syriac Bible, which Vincent did not allow him to do, or in the controversial Hebrew scholar Jacques Corborand de la Fosse. They would be on surer ground with Pierre Collet (1693-1770) who was an intense worker and esteemed theologian. His solid biography of St. Vincent and opposition to Jansenist theology would allow them to experience the level of culture which characterized the best professors of the eighteenth century. They would feel at home with René Rogue who was executed in 1796 and with François and Gruyer who were massacred in 1792. These confreres, beatified by the Church, taught in seminaries and are clearly their colleagues, patrons and advocates.

Closer to our own time, within reach of our hands and hearts, certain Vincentian silhouettes continue this tradition. Pierre Coste, the indefatigable and industrious editor of the works of Vincent, comes to mind; or the old Father Parrang who found new life working in the French National Archives; or the enthusiastic Joseph Guichard; or the tenacious Charles François Jean, who learned Babylonian at age forty-two and taught at L'Ecole du Louvre for the next twenty-five years.

Above all, two "great men," Fernand Portal and Guillaume Pouget, illustrate the vitality of the turn-of-the-century Vincentian contemplative, who let their lives be nurtured by hope and hidden successes. They were born to be mediators.

The first, Fernand Portal, felt himself called to an apostolate of friendship. He was a true ecumenist. Vincent's remark, "One does not believe a person because he is well-educated, but because we consider him good and love him," might have been said of him. He had struck up a friendship with Lord Halifax, which allowed him to engage Catholics and Protestants in an amiable dialogue in the conversations of Malines presided over by Cardinal Mercier. His disciples, Abbot Gratieux, Canon Hemmer and Father Viller, S.J. among many others, were friends who worked together for unity among Christians, the lack of which more than ever haunts contemporary Christianity.

The second "great man," Guillaume Pouget of Auvergne, had an obscure career and the vocation of one who is hidden. Blind, but in love with the light, he astonished people with his fantastic memory. He was a dedicated exegete, a thinker . . . and forgetful of himself. Fortunately, this "Christian Socrates," as Claudel named him, found in Jean Guitton a sympathetic and fascinating Plato. Among those who took pride in having listened to Pouget's advice are Jacques Chevalier, Emmanuel Mounier and Maurice Legendre. They were endlessly amazed at the depths of his secrets of charity.

His meeting with Lord Halifax and his conversations with Henri Bergson remain the events which symbolize and reveal him to have been a mystic of simplicity. Once again, the words of Vincent offer the finest testimony. As Vincent had said of Duval, one could say of Pouget: "Good and holy doctors are the treasures of the Church" (XI, 127).

It is likewise easy to discern the outline of a double tradition in the history of Charity lived by the women of Vincent's family. The first, allied with Saint Louise and Saint Catherine Labouré, honors humble devotion to the Virgin — she, who, as Vincent had said, speaks and prays for those who are not able to speak for themselves.

The second type tends to a social style, which invokes and secretly points to a woman with a great heart, Sister Rosalie Rendu. She was always at the service of the residents of the Mouffetard district of Paris, where she lived more than one hundred years ago and was their advocate until she died. Today invisibly she continues her rounds.

Vincent's Religious Influence

Vincent would have accused himself of being short-sighted and lazy had he been engaged only in working with his two religious communities. So, at his death, he could not abandon the works he supported. His activity on behalf of the religious life of the Church took on new forms.

Charitable Organizations

What became of the charitable organizations that Vincent initiated?

The Ladies of Charity, unable to continue during the French Revolution, experienced a rebirth in the nineteenth century. Today, still under the direction of Saint Vincent de Paul's successor, they have 450,000 members. They are particularly active in Italy, Poland, Belgium, Mexico, Brazil and the United States. In 1911, the Louisettes were founded as a branch of the Ladies of Charity.

In 1833 Frederic Ozanam had the spirit, tenacity and grace to realize Vincent's dream of charities conducted by men. The St. Vincent de Paul Conferences have performed an immense service, in spite of periodic criticism. By 1990, there were 800,000 members in 113 countries on all continents.

Vincent painstakingly continues to aid the poor, fight new forms of sin and hardship and without regret or bitterness discreetly give his advice. One suspects he inspires, supports and protects many of the vast undertakings and initiatives which respond to his vision of assistance to the needy, refugees and the homeless.

New Forms of Religious Life

In relation to religious communities of women, Vincent quietly continues to exercise the role of animator and reformer which he had during his lifetime. No longer able to govern and direct these communities in person, he mystically teaches, forewarns, suggests, counsels. He used to say that Cardinal de Bérulle had taught him the importance of acting as silently and invisibly as angels do.

Thanks to Monsieur Vincent and his tenacity in winning approval of the Constitutions of the Vincentians and the Daughters of Charity, many religious congregations of the seventeenth, eighteenth, and nineteenth centuries were free to adopt new lifestyles, in which monastic practices declined and individual and collective discipline was shaped by the exhausting demands of the modern apostolate. "When you leave prayer to care for the sick," Vincent made clear to the Daughters of Charity, "you will be leaving God for God. To care for the sick is to pray."

These new communities of men and women, whether or not they borrow the Rules from the Missionaries or Daughters of Charity, for example the Sisters of Charity of Clement-August and the Sisters of Tilbourg, or take Saint Vincent as their patron or protector, like the Sisters of Charity of Besançon, the Sisters of Divine Providence of Ribeauville, the Brothers of St. Vincent de Paul of Father Le Prevost and the Sons and Daughters of Charity of Father Anizan, all share the methods and spirit that Saint Vincent envisioned and put into practice.

It was in order to transpose Vincentian charity into other areas that St. Alphonsus Liguori established the Congregation of the Very Holy Redeemer in 1732 and St. John Bosco founded the Salesian Order in 1840.

More than one hundred religious communities steer their own course in the wake of Vincent's small and fragile craft. To the frightened and storm-tossed he still says, "Let us allow God to captain our small boat. The Lord will keep it from capsizing" (cf., V, 448).

Expressions of Faith

Beyond the social structures of religious life, it is in the interior life, the life of the spirit, that Vincent remains especially active and continues his vocation as educator of religious. There is, in fact, an interior life which can be called Vincentian, not because it takes its cues from the rules given by Vincent, but rather because it adopts his views concerning God and people. It takes his ways of prayer and thinking to heart out of a sense of fidelity to his spirit and a feeling of sympathetic kinship. It assimilates his psychology and grows into his practical wisdom. In a word, it seeks to see and fashion its own life in the living mirror of Vincent's spirit.

There are signs that instantly betray its secret attachment to Vincent. It shuns extraordinary forms of religious sentiment. Vincent opposed supernatural phenomena and illusions of all kinds, and was extremely reserved in his conduct toward visionaries and mystical phenomena. If needed, it would be an effective and healthy custom to periodically re-read his conference on illusions. His caution was rooted in personal experience. He was suspicious of extraordinary signs as possible tricks of the devil, to which he knew people were susceptible when exhausted from work. Wasn't there, after all, reason for thinking that ecstasies were often more harmful than useful?

Vincent, opposed to the Jansenistic teachings of Antoine

Arnauld, extolled frequent participation in the eucharist and the sacrament of penance. He recognized these sacraments as sources of healing and signs of excellent spiritual health.

Vincentian interiority juxtaposes two attitudes which seem mutually exclusive. On one hand, it lays claim to intellectual rigor and has concern for the concrete and practical. In this, it transposes Descartes' rigorous and rational *Discourse on Method* to a religious plane. On the other hand, Vincentian faith stubbornly rejects any easy alliance with the treacherous side of human nature. If one were to listen only to human nature, one could believe with Vincent, that religious life would only produce a human blossoming and fail to reach full fruition. It is important "not to fall into the trap." Paradoxically, the peace of Christ develops within a context of opposition and an atmosphere of struggle. The Spirit of God, who lives within the human person, ceaselessly cares for us in the midst of our struggles: zeal and humility, then simplicity and discernment, finally mortification are the weapons of the Spirit.

Thus, Vincent de Paul, in agreement with his friend, Francis de Sales, gives the spiritual lives of his followers a characteristic mark. He reties the knot between religion and action. Spirituality and devotion simultaneously express, demonstrate and prolong the experience of goodness in action.

Devotion to Mary

A notable outcome of fidelity to the principles of Vincentian spiritual life has been a highly developed Marian devotion at the heart of the two religious families of Vincent.

Devotion to Mary was an element in Vincent's first sermons and was evident in the Marian patronage sought by the first Confraternity of Charity in 1617. As the Vincentian family remained faithful to the deepest rhythms of its interior life, devotion to Mary flourished.

Without doubt it benefited from the fervor of the nineteenth century. But, it benefited still more from the apparitions to Saint Catherine Labouré in 1830. Two forms of Marian devotion, centered on the Immaculate Conception, are in full bloom: the Association of the Children of Mary Immaculate and the Novena of the Miraculous Medal. The Association of the Children of Mary Immaculate had 150,000 members in 1960. The Vincentian Marian movement among young people and young adults has been particularly effective and influential in Europe, especially in Spain.

The Novena of the Miraculous Medal has made of the chapel built for the Daughters of Charity at 140 rue de Bac the most frequented place of worship in Paris. In the United States, these devotions claim millions of faithful followers through the apostolic work of the Central Association of the Miraculous Medal in Philadelphia and the National Shrine of the Miraculous Medal in Perryville, Missouri. *La Médaille Miraculeuse*, founded by J. P. Henrion, has had a large readership over the years.

"When the Mother of God is invoked and taken as patroness of important matters, how could anything not go well and give glory to her son Jesus!" (XIV, 126).

The Legend of Vincent and Heart Values

To know Monsieur Vincent it is not enough to describe his acts of service and know his religious influence. In the popular imagination, where his memory is kept alive, Vincent de Paul was "a great man." Ordinary people remembered him as a man who possessed the humanity which Richelieu lacked, and lacked the cunning of the unlovable Mazarin. The Vincent whom the people remembered had a smile of simple goodness and transparent kindness.

Vincent deserved his reputation for kindness. The best proof of it came perhaps from the way his own conscience reproached him for even the slightest harshness to others.

Only tenderhearted people are this sensitive to callousness. He begged God to imprint on his heart pure and tender love. "Let it [this tender love] be," he added, "the life of my life and the soul of my actions." He kept guard over his exterior and advised: "It's important to be appealing and have a face which doesn't frighten anyone" (XII,189). A frequent subject of his prayer was the special gift given by God to some people: "the gift of being cordial, pleasant, kind, present and accessible to all, a gift by which they seem to offer their hearts and ask for yours" (XII, 189).

The pictures and biographies of Vincent are authentic in the degree they let us see the quality of his soul and the love which filled it. It is a fact that during the more than three hundred years since his death, there has been an ongoing love affair between him and humanity. Yet, today as in his own time, he can be ignored by some, be a bother to others and even call forth disdain. He did not always win everyone's sympathy, even though he wasn't ever bitterly detested or hated. He experienced opposition, both from the people involved in Jansenism at Port-Royal and from others unhappy with him. Mixed up in public affairs, there was no way he could escape being splashed with political mud. Given his life, it was impossible for him to be the object of universal and unconditional affection. Even the compliments and official thanks addressed to him sometimes masked the barbs of selfish interests. When aid and alms diminished, kindly sentiments dried up and he then sometimes encountered hot anger. He was openly insulted when supplies and food were scarce at the time of the Fronde. Yet, his death grieved everyone.

With his death began an era in which his image was polished and idealized. It was only with the passage of time that others were able to picture him according to the real feelings of the people.

In the eighteenth century popular devotion to Vincent had a particularly sentimental cast to it. He was held up as someone to be admired. Perrault (1770) placed him in the company of illustrious men and women. Even his beatification and canonization exalted him as a religious model and heavenly patron, this man who was the Father of the Poor. All these official honors, however, would have been dead letters without the widespread and heartfelt devotion of the people, who preserved the sentiment and human character of Vincent's spirit. The image of Vincent as the Father of his Country, the friend of galley slaves and the protector of refugees breathed real life into his otherwise spiritualized and idealized figure. In an era which fervently distrusted rich and tyrannical power, Vincent appeared extremely attractive.

Over time he benefited also from the neutral character of his portraits. They did not portray him as a revolutionary character nor, on the other hand, as a sanctimonious person or someone who stayed in church. Some portraits show him dressed in a surplice, others, however, in a shabby winter coat. He was represented as someone with whom people felt at ease in the welcoming warmth of good company. He was approachable and talked easily with people, so it wasn't long before he was portrayed with other people (1717). His vocation to go to all was exploited to such an extent, that people forgot he ever preached, conducted missions or heard confessions. These pictures represented him exclusively in intimate conversation or as posing for posterity engaged in a work of charity. In all these scenes the church is never far away, usually represented by a bell tower in the background. But it was the poor who were always in the foreground at center stage.

The tradition of seeing Vincent as a great man detached from his historical context began in the eighteenth century and continues into the present time. Such an image was perfectly acceptable to ordinary people and those who suffered. They didn't care about the scholarly questions. It also suited the religious sentiments of Voltaire and eventually the Revolutionaries. Along with Fénelon and Ben Franklin, Vincent was honored as a "Great Benefactor of Humanity." With that accolade his embalming was complete.

Between 1790 and 1800 Vincent's portraits lost their vitality. The softness of his features aimed at showing his goodness, but only succeeded in making him appear anonymous and average. In place of a portrait we were given an idealized image, the national hero replaced the man of God.

Romanticism then had a field day. Sculptors, engravers and illustrators competed with one another. Poet historians gave their imaginations free rein. Cappefigue in 1827, for example, created a touching journal of a Daughter of Charity, who each day recorded the nightly forays of Saint Vincent. The tapestry of Vincent's great charitable works was embroidered with moralizing stories. To foster a certain type of piety among children and pious folks Vincent's conversations with torturers, convicts and poor people were reconstructed with an innocence and naivete which eliminated hardships. The glory of Alembert, abandoned as a child and saved from the streets, shone romantically on all abandoned children, suggesting for each of them unsuspected future greatness. The prolific literature of the time focused on three expressions of Vincent's work: foundlings, galley slaves and those in need of help, especially victims of war. The rest of Vincent's work was consciously forgotten. For these three works, however, there was a festival of pictures, words and warm feelings.

Pierre Fresnay continued this image of Vincent for moviegoers in Maurice Cloche's 1947 film. He gave Vincent a look of fire and a strong, sonorous voice. He surrounded him with his legendary friends — foundlings, galley slaves and refugees. There was no possible doubt: this was indeed Vincent and this is who Vincent was. He even spoke the language of Jean Anouilh correctly.

Historians who critiqued the legend were still able to find consolation in the fact that the Vincent of history was the source of the Vincent of legend. Yet, they had to admit that it is the popular image of Vincent which continues to fire the imagination of millions of people after three centuries. Awkwardly perhaps but as a matter of fact, the man of legend is the object of people's daily affection and thoughts and is the one to whom they address their prayers. Their image of him concretizes and protects the imperishable values of the heart. The legendary Vincent is the same as Monsieur Vincent, because Vincent is not only the man who lived from 1581 to 1660, but also the one whose spirit invites each of us to follow and become a human person living heart and soul in God's love.

Goodbye

"He practically changed the face of the Church," declared Bishop Henri de Maupas du Tour on November 23, 1660, in the first funeral eulogy for Vincent de Paul. What would the face of the Church have been without his life and works? No one knows. It would only be speculation if one dared to imagine it. It does not matter!

Vincent simply invites us to pay attention to his life. We are certain of this: he never succeeded in getting his "early retirement." Yet, in his twilight years he did retire into the crevices of humanity's conscience.

From time to time, he awakens quietly. He comes to us humbly. He does not reproach us or give us a sermon. He is one of God's poor, delightfully simple, poor. He comes that we might still believe that the Christ infinitely surpasses our human ways. He begs for our love.

Birthplace of St. Vincent de Paul (near Dax)

The Church of Châtillon-des-Dombes (today known as Châtillon-sur-Chalaronne, Ain).

As early as 1664, Abelly suggested that M. Vincent, while visiting convicts, would have removed iron chains from one of them (print made from a painting of Bonnat).

Letter of M. Vincent to Louise de Marillac (1638-1639, I, 493). One of more than 400 that have been preserved. (23)

Louise de Marillac

Sicut misit me Pater, et Ego mitto vos. Io.20.

Circuibant per Castella Euangelizantes &c. Luc.9

Christ sending his apostles and missionaries to continue the mission with the poor (frontispiece on the first edition of the Rules and Constitutions, 1658).

The Lord of Charity (at the Daughters of Charity Motherhouse).

Sancta Trinitas vnus Deus

Verbum caro factum est.

REGLES ou CONSTITVTIÕS COMMVNES de la CONGREGATION de la MISSION A PARIS 1658

O salutaris hostia.

Et erat subditus illis. Luc. 2.

Cover of the first French edition of the Rules. It is the only book M. Vincent considered himself the author of . . . after God.

Ritratto inedito di San Vincenzo de Paoli. Scoperto alla Biblioteca Mazzarino di Parigi nel 1977. Autore ignoto.

A sketch of Vincent made during his lifetime, but only discovered in 1977 in the Mazarin Library in Paris.

Print taken from the "Rule of Perfection" of Benet of Canfield.

Monsieur Vincent as portrayed by Pierre Fresnay (film of Maurice Cloche).

Early Portrait

Left: Portrait of M. Vincent in street clothes, by François Simon de Tours.
Right: Portrait of M. Vincent in choir clothes, by François Simon de Tours.

Nicolas Pitau

Van Schuppen

René Lochon

Gérard Edelinck

Early Portraits

LOOKING FOR A GOOD RETIREMENT

1581-1608

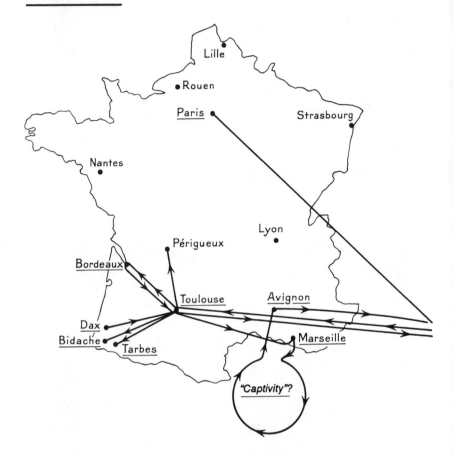

While Vincent was looking for a good and early retirement, God was writing straight with curved and broken lines.

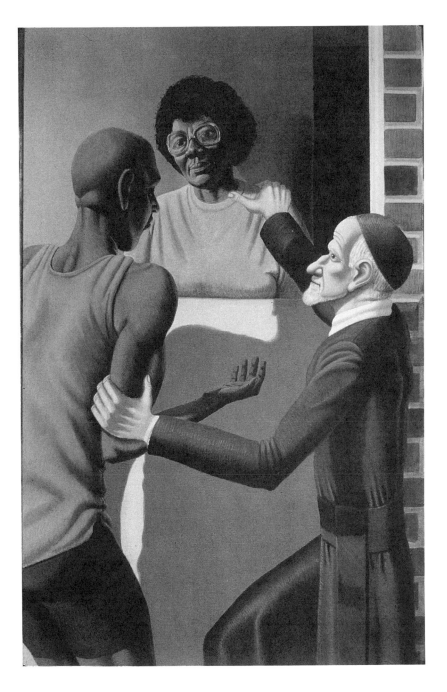

Painting by Brother Mark Elder, C.M. (owned by Richard Ryan, C.M.)

Photo taken at the Rue du Bac of a man on his way to the chapel of the Miraculous Medal.

A Typical Day in the Life of Vincent

Prayer: 3 hours; work: 9.5 hours; miscellaneous: 4.5 hours; sleep: 7 hours

4:00 A.M.	Rising
4:30	Prayer
5:30	Mass
	Personal Work
10:30	Self-examination and Meal
11:30	Break
12:30 P.M.	Personal Work
2:00	Vespers
	Personal Work
5:00	Matins
5:45	Supper
6:15	Break
7:15	Personal Work
9:00	Sleep

Texts[1]

Guidelines for the young Father Antione Durand, when appointed superior of Agde Seminary, 1656

Father Antione Durand, who was born in 1629, was a member of the upper class. On entering the Congregation he was sent to Poland where he was ordained a priest in 1654. He was only twenty-seven years old when Vincent appointed him the superior of the House of Agde and gave him the following guidelines for sound spiritual leadership.

Father Durand's youth and the importance of his new responsibility explain the precision and detail of Vincent's letter to him as well as the variety of topics covered. Through this letter we get a picture of Vincent's view of spiritual leadership. Vincent points out the excellence of the ministry of spiritual guidance and leadership. He bases himself upon the example of the Lord Jesus. Then he recalls that in order to continue the work of Jesus a person has to put on the spirit of humility and let the Son of God act through him. Finally the superior has to know how to care for the material needs of his confreres as well as the spiritual in imitation of God's providential care for all things.

O Monsieur, how great, how very great, is the task of governing souls to which God is calling you! What a great

---

1. The principal source of these texts is Pierre Coste, *Saint Vincent de Paul: Correspondance, Entretiens, Documents* (Paris, 1920-25) 14 vols. It is cited simply by volume (Roman) and page (Arabic). The first three volumes are cited from the current English translation (New York: New City Press, 1985-   ) and indicated as ET.

80

vocation is that of the priests of the Mission who are bound to guide and govern souls, whose secrets God alone knows! "Guiding souls is the art of arts. . . ." It was the task of the Son of God when he was on earth. It was to this he devoted every moment of his life and, in the end, suffered a most painful death. Hence you should conceive a high esteem of that which you are now about to do.

But what are the means of acquitting oneself of this task of guiding souls to God? How can you erect a dam against the torrent of the vices of a people and of the faults and failings of a seminary? How can you inspire feelings for the Christian and ecclesiastical virtues of those whom Providence confides to your care, so that you may contribute to their salvation or perfection? Surely, Monsieur, there is no human element in that; it is not a human work but God's. "A grand work. . ." It is to continue the labors of Jesus Christ. And hence human industry is here of no avail unless God is intimately united with it. No, Monsieur, neither philosophy, nor theology, nor discourses influence souls. It is essential that Jesus Christ be intimately united with us or we with him; that we operate in him and he in us; that we speak like him and in his spirit as he himself was in his Father and preached the doctrine taught him by the Father. That is what holy scripture teaches us.

It is therefore, Monsieur, essential for you to be empty of self in order to put on Jesus Christ. You know that like produces like, a sheep begets a sheep and a human being another human being. So too, if he who guides others, who forms them, who speaks to them, is only animated by a human spirit, those who will see, hear and study to imitate him will become utterly human. No matter what he may say or do, he will inspire them only with the appearance but not the reality. He will communicate to them the spirit with which he himself is animated, as we see in the case of teachers who imprint their maxims and methods of work on their disciples.

On the other hand, if a superior is filled with God, if he is replenished with the maxims of Jesus Christ, all his words will prove efficacious, and a power will go out from him which will edify. All his actions will be salutary instructions, which will work good in those who know about them.

To reach that stage, Monsieur, it is essential that our Lord himself impress his mark and character upon you. Just as a wild stock on which a seedling has been grafted brings forth fruits of the same sort as the seedling, so too with us, poor creatures. When our Lord imprints his mark on us and gives us, so to say, the sap of his spirit and grace, we, being united to him as the branches are united to the vine, will do what he did when he was on earth. I mean to say, we shall perform divine actions and beget, like Saint Paul, beings filled with this spirit, children to our Lord.

Prayer

An important point, and one to which you should carefully devote yourself, is to establish a close union between yourself and our Lord in prayer. That is the reservoir in which you will receive the instructions you need to fulfill the duties on which you are now about to enter. When in doubt, have recourse to God and say to him: "O Lord, you are the Father of light, teach me what I ought to do in this circumstance."

I give you this advice not only for those difficulties which will cause you pain, but also that you may learn from God directly what you shall have to teach, following the example of Moses who proclaimed to the people of Israel only that with which God had inspired him: "The Lord says this."

Moreover, you should have recourse to God in prayer that you may preserve your soul in his fear and love. I am bound to tell you, and you should know it, persons are often lost while contributing to the salvation of others. An individual may do well in his own room and yet forget himself when engaged in external occupations. Saul was found worthy to be king because he led a good life in his father's house. And yet, after he had been raised to the throne he fell away

miserably from the grace of God. Saint Paul chastised his body
in the fear that, after having preached to others and pointed
out to them the way of salvation, he might become a castaway.

Now, if you are not to fall into the wretched state of Saul,
or of Judas, you must attach yourself inseparably to our Lord
and, raising your heart and mind to him frequently, say: "O
Lord, do not allow me, while wishing to save others, to be
miserably lost. Be my shepherd and refuse me not the graces
which you communicated to others through me and my
ministry."

You should have recourse to prayer also to beseech our
Lord to provide for the needs of those entrusted to your
charge. Rest assured that you will gather more fruit in this way
than by any other. Jesus Christ, who is the exemplar of all your
conduct, was not content with sermons, labors, fasts and even
his blood and death itself, but he also added prayer to all that.
He had no need whatsoever of prayer for himself. It was for
us that he prayed so fervently and also to teach us to do the
same, both in regards to all that concerns ourselves and all
that concerns those of whom we should be, with him, the
saviors.

Humility

Another thing I commend to you is the humility of our Lord.
Say frequently: "O Lord, what have I done to be entrusted with
such a task? What deeds have I that correspond with the
burden you have laid on my shoulders? Ah! My God, I would
spoil everything if you did not direct all my words and actions." Let us always contemplate in ourselves what is human
and imperfect, and we shall find only too much matter for
self-humiliation, not only in the sight of God but also in that
of the people and those who are our subjects.

Above all, shun the desire of appearing to be a superior or
a master. I do not agree with the person who said to me some
time ago that a man must demonstrate his superiority, if he is

to rule properly and maintain his authority. O my God, our Lord Jesus Christ never spoke like that. He taught us the contrary by word and example, telling us that he had not come to be served but to serve others, and that he who wishes to be master should be the servant of all.

Therefore, embrace that holy maxim and act toward those with whom you are about to live "as one among them," telling them from the first that you have not come to be their master but to serve them well. Do that both inside and outside the house and you will benefit from it. Furthermore, we should always refer to God whatever good has been accomplished by our endeavors and, on the other hand, attribute to ourselves all the evil that occurs in the community. Yes, remember that all disorders principally proceed from the superior, who, by his negligence or bad example, introduces irregularity, just as all the members of the body languish when the head is unwell.

Humility should also induce you to shun all self-complacency, which insinuates itself in all activities that have an element of glory in them. O Monsieur, how poisonous vain complacency is to good works. It is a plague which corrupts the holiest actions and makes a person quickly forget God. Be on your guard, in the name of God, against this failing, as in my opinion it is one of the most dangerous to progress in the spiritual life and perfection.

Therefore, give yourself to God so that you may speak in the humble spirit of Jesus Christ, confessing that your doctrine is neither your own nor from yourself but the teaching of the gospel. Above all imitate the simplicity of language and of simile and metaphor which our Lord uses in holy scripture when speaking to the people. What wonderful things he might have taught them! What secrets of the Divine Nature and its adorable perfections might he not have revealed, he who was the Eternal Wisdom of the Father! And yet, you see how plainly he speaks, and how he employs homely comparisons, such as that of a husbandman, a vine-dresser, a field, a vineyard, a grain of mustard seed. That is how you should speak if you wish people to whom you announce the word of God to understand you.

Imitation of Our Lord

Another point to which you should pay particular attention is to depend greatly on the guidance of the Son of God. I mean to say, when you have to act, you should reflect like this: "Is this in conformity with the maxims of the Son of God?" If not, say: "I will have nothing to do with it," but if you find that it is, say, "Very well, let us do it."

Moreover, whenever there is question of doing a good work, say to the Son of God: "O Lord, if you were in my place, what would you do? How would you instruct the people? How would you console this illness of body or mind?"

This dependence should also be extended to manifesting great deference to those who represent our Lord to you and who hold the place of your superiors. Believe me, their experience and the grace which Jesus Christ in his goodness communicates to them have taught them a great deal about government. I am telling you this in order to induce you not to do anything of importance nor to undertake anything out of the ordinary without letting us know about it or, if the matter is so urgent that you have not time to wait for our solution, consult the nearest superior and say to him: "Monsieur, what would you do on such an occasion?" We have experienced that God has blessed the leadership of those who have acted in this way, whereas those who have acted otherwise have involved themselves in affairs which not only have caused themselves a great deal of trouble but have also proved embarrassing to us.

I also beg you to take care not to have any desire to govern in any unusual way. I wish you not to be peculiar in any respect, but always to follow the *viam regiam*,[2] the main road, so that you may walk surely and blamelessly. By this I

2. Literally the royal road, that is, the highway.

mean that you should conform in every respect to the rules and holy customs of the Congregation. Make no innovations but bear in mind the instructions that have been drawn up for those charged with the government of the houses of the Company and do not eliminate any of those things that are carried on in our Company.

Be faithful not only in the observance of the rules but in seeing that they are observed because, if you do not, all will go badly. And as you hold the place of the Lord, so you should after his example be a light which enlightens and warms. "Jesus Christ," says Saint Paul, "is the splendor of the Father," and Saint John tells us that he is the light which enlightens every person who comes into the world.

We see that higher causes influence those that are lower. For instance, angels of a superior hierarchy enlighten, illumine and perfect intelligences of a lower hierarchy. So the superior, pastor and director should purify, illuminate and unite with God the souls committed to his charge by God himself.

And as the heavens have a kindly influence upon the earth so those who are placed over others should pour forth on them the spirit with which they themselves are animated. To do so, you should be utterly replenished with grace, light and good works, just as we see the sun communicating the fullness of its brightness to the other stars.

Finally, you should be like salt, "You are the salt of the earth," and prevent corruption from attacking the flock of which you are to be the shepherd.

(After Monsieur Vincent had with a zeal and charity I cannot express, said to me all that has been set down above, a lay-brother came in and spoke to him about some temporal matter affecting the house of Saint-Lazare. When the brother left, he took advantage of the circumstance to give me the following advice.)

You see, Monsieur, how I must pass from the things of God, of which we were speaking just now, to temporal matters?

From this you should learn that it is the duty of a superior to provide not only for spiritual things but also to extend his care to temporal ones. As those whom he has to guide are composed of body and soul, so he is bound to provide for the needs of both one and the other after the example of God the Father, who is engaged from all eternity in begetting his Son, from whom, with the Father, the Holy Spirit proceeds. Apart from those divine operations *ad intra*, he has created the world *ad extra* and is continually engaged in preserving it and all those things that depend upon it, and in producing ever new crops in the earth, new fruit on the trees, etc. The same adorable Providence is at work to such a degree that a leaf does not fall from the tree without his orders. God numbers all the hairs of our head and provides food for the smallest little grub, yes, even for a flesh worm. This seems to me to be a very powerful consideration for enabling you to understand that you should devote yourself not only to that which is noble, such as functions concerned with spiritual matters, but also, as a superior who represents in a manner the full compass of the power of God, you should apply yourself to the care of the smallest temporal affairs, reminding yourself that such care is not unworthy of you. Give yourself to God then to procure the temporal prosperity of the community to which you are going.

The Son of God, when he first sent out his apostles, told them not to take money with them but afterwards, when the number of his disciples had increased, it was his will that there should be one of his band who should not only feed the poor but provide for the needs of his band. Furthermore, he permitted women to follow him for the same purpose, "who administered to him." If he tells us in the gospel to take no care for tomorrow, this should be interpreted as not being too anxious or solicitous about temporal goods rather than absolutely to neglect the means of keeping alive and of clothing oneself, otherwise, people would not even sow seed.

I shall now finish. It is enough for today. I now repeat that

you are about to undertake a great work, *grande opus.* I beg
our Lord to bless your leadership and beseech him, on your
part and on mine, to forgive me for all the faults I have
committed in the task on which I am engaged.

(XI, 342-51 - ET: Leonard, *Conferences of Saint Vincent de Paul*
[Philadelphia, 1963], 323-30).

Instructions and Guidance

Christ

Remember, Monsieur, we live in Jesus Christ through the
death of Jesus Christ, and we die in Jesus Christ through the
life of Jesus Christ. Our life must be hidden in Jesus Christ and
filled with Jesus Christ. In order to die as Jesus Christ, we must
live as Jesus Christ. Once these foundations have been laid,
let us give ourselves up to contempt, to shame, to ignominy,
and let us disclaim the honors people pay us, the good
reputation and the applause they give us, and let us do nothing
which has not that end in view.

(To Antoine Portail, May 1, 1635 - ET: I, 276)

I pray our Lord himself will be your strength and life, as he
is for all those who feed upon his love.

(To Edmund Jolly, Priest of the Mission,
July 11, 1659 - VIII, 15)

I am edified . . . by the view the Lord is giving you of your
poverty. . . . Nevertheless, be careful not to rule others by your
self, but rather through the Lord who has capacity enough for
you and him. I ask him to animate you with that part of his spirit
which gives humility, kindness, support, patience, vigilance,
prudence, and charity. You will find all these virtues in him,
and if you allow him, he will make them work in you and
through us. Live trusting him, and remain at peace.

(To Guillaume Desdames, Priest of the Mission,
January 30, 1660 - VIII, 231)

Should not we give ourselves to him at this moment to please him in order to act from now on in him and through him? *Deus virtutum*, he is the God of virtues.

(Conference to the Missionaries, March 7, 1659 - XII, 154)

Human actions become actions of God when they are performed in him and through him.

(Conference to the Missionaries,
March 28, 1659 - XII, 183)

I beg the Lord to renew all of you in his Spirit, so that all your undertakings will belong to him and the fruits obtained will lead you to eternal life.

(To Jean Martin, Priest of the Mission,
July 30, 1660 - VIII, 333)

I commend myself to your prayers and also commend the Little Company so that the Lord might accomplish his holy will in it and through it.

(To Guillaume Desdames, Priest of the Mission,
August 3, 1660 - VIII, 424)

Jesus Christ is the rule of the Mission.

(Conference to the Missionaries,
February 21, 1659 - XII, 130)

Our Lord has all virtues in abundance . . . but they are not in him for himself. They are for all those whom he uses in his works and who place all their confidence in his help.

(To Edmund Jolly, Priest of the Mission,
December 17, 1655 - V, 484)

Do not limit your vision any longer to yourself, but see the Lord around you and in you, ready to put his hand to the work as soon as you ask for his help. You will see that all will go well.

(To Louis Rivet, Priest of the Mission,
December 19, 1655 - V, 488)

We cannot better assure our eternal happiness than by living and dying in the service of the poor and in the arms of Providence, genuinely renouncing ourselves in order to follow Jesus Christ.

(To Jean Barrean, December 4, 1648 - ET:
III, 384)

Our Lord Jesus Christ is the meek master of human beings and of angels. By the practice of this same virtue of meekness you will go to him and bring others to him as well.

(Abelly, ET: III, 168)

The more our actions and sufferings resemble those of Christ's on earth, the more pleasing they are to God. And as your imprisonment honors God, the Lord of heaven honors you with his patience, in which I pray he will confirm you.

(To Brother Jean Barreau, September 16, 1650 - IV, 81)

Our Lord Jesus Christ is our father, our mother and our all.

(To Nicholas Etienne, Priest of the Mission,
January 30, 1656 - V, 534)

I pray our Lord that he will be the life of our life and the only desire of our hearts.

(To Charles Ozenne, Priest of the Mission,
October 26, 1657 - VI, 563)

One way to ensure the continuing blessings of the Lord is to use them as soon as we receive them, according to his good pleasure for the greatest benefit to our neighbor.

(To Pierre Cabel, Priest of the Mission,
November 22, 1659 - VIII, 178)

The reputation of the Company is in Jesus Christ, and the way to maintain it is to imitate him, not famous preachers.

(To Gabriel Delespiney, Missionary, October 17, 1659
- VIII, 149)

Nothing pleases me, but in Jesus Christ.

(Abelly, ET: I, chapter 19)

The second maxim of this faithful servant of God was always to see our Savior Jesus Christ in others, to inspire our charity toward them. In the Holy Father, the pope, he saw our divine Savior as pontiff and head of the Church. The bishop he saw as Jesus the bishop and prince of pastors. He saw the doctors of the Church as Jesus the religious, the king as Jesus the sovereign ruler, gentlemen as Jesus the noble one, magistrates, governors, and other officers as Jesus the judge and all-wise ruler. In the gospel the kingdom of heaven is compared to a merchant, and so it was that he looked on traders. He saw Jesus the worker in the artisans, Jesus the poor one in the poor, Jesus suffering in the sick and dying. He looked on all states in life, seeing in each the image of his sovereign Lord who dwelt in the person of his neighbor. He was moved, in this view, to honor, respect, love, and serve each person as our Lord, and our Lord in each individual. He wanted his followers and all those with whom he spoke to enter into these same sentiments, to make their charity toward the neighbor more constant and more perfect.

(Abelly, ET: I, 107)

The Will of God

It could be said this conformity of his own will to the will of God was the moving force and the overriding virtue of this holy man, shedding its light on all his other virtues. It was the master virtue controlling all the other faculties of his soul and even of his body. It was the prime motive of his exercises of piety, of all the holy practices of religion, and of all his actions.

(Abelly, ET: III, 40)

Be then his dear daughter—quite humble, submissive, and full of confidence—and always wait patiently for the manifestation of his holy and adorable will.

(To Louise de Marillac, October 30, 1626 - ET: I, 24)

Be quite cheerful in the disposition of willing everything that God wills. And since it is his good pleasure that we remain always in the holy joy of his love, let us remain in it and attach ourselves to it inseparably in this world, so that we may one day be one in him, in whose love I am, Mademoiselle, your most humble and obedient servant.

(To Louise de Marillac, February 9, 1628 - ET: I, 36)

You are wrong, my dear daughter, in thinking that I was of the opinion that you should not accept the young lady's suggestion, because I have not given it a thought. And I have not given it a thought, because I am sure that you will and do not will what God wills and does not will, and that you are disposed to want and not want only what you recognize that God seems to want and not want.

(undated, c. 1626-29 - I, 54)

Mon Dieu, my daughter, what great hidden treasures there are in holy Providence and how marvelously our Lord is honored by those who follow it and do not try to get ahead of it! Yes, you will tell me, but it is on account of God that you are worried. It is no longer because of God that you are worried, if you are troubled because of serving him.

(To Louise de Marillac, C. 1629 - ET: I, 59)

Our Lord will perhaps draw more glory from your submission than from all the good you might do. One beautiful diamond is worth more than a mountain of stones, and one virtuous act of acquiescence and submission is better than an abundance of good works done for others.

(To Louise de Marillac, April, 1630 - ET: I, 75)

Vincent later gave the same advice to Father Bernard Codoing, Priest of the Mission, whose feverish zeal caused him to neglect the care of his community in favor of premature and often inopportune projects.

In the name of God, Monsieur, stop being concerned about things happening far away that are none of your business, and devote all your attention to domestic discipline. The rest will come in due time. Grace has its moments. Let us abandon ourselves to the Providence of God and be on our guard against anticipating it. If our Lord is pleased to give any consolation in my vocation, it is that we have it seems to me tried to follow divine Providence in all things and to put our feet only on the paths Providence has marked out for us.

(March 16, 1644 - ET: II, 499)

We will, therefore, not send Sisters to Champigny, because no one seems in favor of it. I fear however that you did not allow Providence a free hand, but attempted something she did not want. My God, Monsieur, how good it is to trust her on these occasions, without wanting to anticipate her orders!

(June 22, 1650 - IV, 34)

God's Providence is responsible for these affairs [establishing a house in Lombardy]. We must not desire nor search out any other way by ourselves or through others. The custom of the Company has always been to wait for, and not anticipate, the orders from on high.

(To Edmund Jolly, November 29, 1658 - VII, 385-86)

Holiness and perfection are defined by conformity to the will of God.

In any case, God will provide for the child and for your son as well, without you giving way to anxiety about what will become of him. Give the child and the mother to our Lord. He will take good care of you and your son. Just let him do his

will in you and in him, and await it in all your exercises. All
you need to do is to devote yourself entirely to God. Oh! How
little it takes to be very holy only to do the will of God in all
things.

(To Louise de Marillac, undated - ET: II, 47)

Perfection does not consist in ecstasies but in doing the will
of God.

(To Missionaries, October 17, 1655 - XI, 317)

We must sanctify our works by seeking God in them and
by doing them in order to find him in them, rather than just
to get them done.

(To Missionaries, February 21, 1659 - XII, 132)

As you know the masters of the spiritual life have proposed
different exercises, which in fact are practiced differently by
different people. Some are very subtle. The shortest way,
though, is the practice of doing God's will in everything. It is
more excellent than everything else, because it includes
indifference, purity of intention, and all the other ways and
practices suggested. If there are other exercises which lead
to perfection, they will surely be found in this one.

(To Missionaries, March 7, 1659 - XII, 152)

The following article [of the Rules] on the will of God,
which is the soul of the Company and one of the practices it
must have foremost at heart, gives each of us an easy, excellent, and infallible way to perfection that makes our actions
no longer human nor angelic, but actions of God because they
are done in him and by him.

(To Missionaries, March 28, 1659 - XII, 183)

What is holiness? It is separation and withdrawal from
earthly things and at the same time affection for God and
union with the divine will.

(To Missionaries, August 22, 1659 - XII, 300)

Apostolic results do not depend upon the intensity of human effort or the multiplicity of activities, but only upon conformity to the will of God. If we wish to act truly and to do much, it is enough simply to do the will of God. Then God accomplishes more than we would have even dreamed of being able to do and he takes care of "our" business because we are doing his.

In the name of God, Monsieur, pay attention to this. Let us reflect that we shall always do God's will and he will do ours, when we carry out that of our superiors. We fall into thousands of difficulties and disorders when we act otherwise.

(To Bernard Codoing, March 17, 1642 - ET: II, 267)

You are fortunate, Monsieur, to be so busy with your duty and, consequently, to be doing God's will, that you have no time to think of yourself. He thinks about you enough and looks after the affairs of your soul while you look after those of your vocation, in which I ask him to bless you more and more.

(To a Missionary - ET: II, 459)

Let us truly belong to God, Monsieur. He will be ours entirely, and in him we shall have all things.

(To Hugues Perraud, July 4, 1649 - ET: III, 459)

In the name of God, Monsieur, let us be more careful to extend the empire of Jesus Christ than our own possessions. Let us take care of his affairs and he will take care of ours. Let us honor his poverty, at least by our moderation, if we do not do so by total imitation.

(To Jacques Chiroye, January 9, 1650 - ET: III, 527)

Allow yourself to be led by the Lord. He will direct all things through you. Trust him and, following his example, always act humbly, gently and in good faith. You will see everything will go well. I know your responsibilities which are many

continue to grow, while your strength diminishes because of
sickness in you and around you. It is God who allows all this
to happen, but believe that he will not leave a heavy burden
on your back without sustaining you. He will be your strength
as well as your reward for the extraordinary services you give
him in this emergency. Three can do more than ten when the
Lord puts his hand to it, and he always does so when he takes
away the means of doing it in another way.

> (To Marc Coglee, Priest of the Mission,
> December 4, 1650 - IV, 115-116)

God be praised that you now have hope of receiving five
hundred pounds for your local needs! Allow God to give it to
us! His Providence never fails us as long as we continue in his
service.

> (To Gilbert Cussot, Priest of the Mission,
> December 9, 1651 - IV, 282)

The good Lord always takes care of our business when we
take care of his.

> (To Jacques Pesnelle, Priest of the Mission,
> November 8, 1658 - VII, 348)

Please hold as infallible the prophetic word first pronounced by Jesus Christ and recently by the Cardinal of
Genoa, that, if you continue to seek God's glory and establish
his reign in souls through your vocation—with the same spirit
which until now seems to be in the Company—you will not
lack anything. May it please God to fill all of us with this same
conviction so we might totally give ourselves to his Providence and service!

> (To Jacques Pesnelle, Priest of the Mission,
> April 4, 1659 - VII, 478)

If we do his business, he will do ours. Let us seek his glory,
let this be our occupation, and let us not trouble ourselves
about anything else. "All those other things which you need

shall be given you in addition." Let us be concerned that God reign in us and in others by means of all the virtues. For temporal things, let us leave to him the care of them—he wills it so. Yes, he will furnish us with food, clothing, and even with learning.

(To Missionaries, February 21, 1659 - XII, 139)

A portrait of the person who follows Providence and does God's will.

I pray God two or three times every day that he will do away with us, if we do not contribute to his glory.

(To Missionaries - XI, 2)

I fell seriously ill two or three days ago, which made me think about death. By the grace of God, I adore God's will and acquiesce in it with all my heart. And on examining myself as to what might cause me some anxiety, I found nothing except that we have not yet drawn up our rules.

(Recipient unknown, c. 1635 - ET: I, 272-73)

Shall I dare to tell you something without blushing, Monsieur? I cannot help it. I must do so. Reflecting on all the principal events that have taken place in this Company, it seems to me to be quite evident, that, if they had taken place before they did, they would not have been successful. I say it of all of them, without excepting a single one. That is why I have a particular devotion to following the adorable Providence of God step by step. My only consolation is that I think our Lord alone has carried on and is constantly carrying on the business of the Little Company. In the name of God, Monsieur, let us take refuge in this, trusting that our Lord will bring about what he wishes to be done among us.

(To Bernard Codoing, December 7, 1641
- ET: II, 236-237)

The consolation our Lord gives me is to believe that, by the grace of God, we have always tried to follow and not to anticipate Providence, which knows how to wisely conduct all things to the end our Lord destines for them. In truth, Monsieur, I have never more clearly seen the vanity of acting contrary to this, nor the meaning of the saying that God uproots the vine that he himself has not planted.

(To Bernard Codoing, April 14, 1644
- ET: II, 502)

This morning, in my feeble prayers, a great desire came upon me of willing everything that happens in the world both good and evil, general as well as particular, because God wills it since he sends it. Oh! How this practice seems to me to have marvellous benefits which would help Missionaries! Let us strive then to have this disposition of will toward the will of God and we will find much good will come, not least of all, among its many benefits, peace of mind.

(To a Missionary - VI, 476)

Notice the holy dispositions in which he lives and the blessings which accompany all he does. He is committed to God, to him alone, and God leads him in everything and by everything. He could say with the prophet: "With your counsel you guide me, and in the end you will receive me in glory." God holds him, so to speak, by his right hand, and he accepts this divine guidance with complete submission. For tomorrow, the following week, the whole year, and his entire life, you will see him living in peace and tranquility, and in an uninterrupted movement toward God. Everywhere he spreads in the souls of his neighbor the happy spirit with which he himself is filled. If you compare him with those who follow their own inclinations you will see how filled with light he is, how fruitful in his work. He makes notable progress, and all his words have strength and energy. God blesses all his undertakings and accomplishes by his grace the designs God has for him. The advice he gives to others and all his actions give great edification. On the other hand, when we look at those attached to their own inclinations and pleasure, their thoughts are worldly, their words those of slaves, and their works lifeless. All this comes from their being attached to creatures. These allow nature to influence their souls while grace acts in those who raise their hearts to God and aspire only to accomplish his will.

(Abelly, ET: III, 47)

If God is the center of your life, no words will be needed. Your mere presence will touch their hearts.

(Abelly, II, chapter 5)

Our Lord is a continual communion for those who are united to what he wills and does not will.

(To Louise de Marillac, C. March, 1634 - ET:
I, 233)

Charity

Definition

Vincent de Paul defined Charity dynamically in terms of the love God gives us and the love we show him from the heart.

Loving someone is wanting all that is good for that person. Loving the Lord then is wanting that his name be known and manifested to the whole world, that his kingdom come and his will be done on earth as it is in heaven.

(Conference to the Daughters of Charity
on the Love of God, [no date] - XI, 43)

To love God above all things means to love him more than anything else, more than father, mother, friends, relations or any created being whatsoever. It is to love him more than oneself. If anything should arise contrary to his glory and his

will, or, if it were necessary to die for him, it would be far, far
better to die than to act against his glory and his pure love.

(Conference to the Daughters of Charity, July 19, 1640
- IX, 19 - ET: Leonard, I, 17)[3]

Charity leads us to God. Charity causes us to love with the
whole range of our affections, to desire that God be loved and
served by all, that people know and love this eternal Truth,
Immensity, Purity, Goodness, Wisdom, Divine Providence,
and that Eternity in which God communicates glory to the
blessed and which causes prayers to be offered continually
for all the world. Those, my dear Sisters, are the effects of
charity toward God, and Sisters who live in this way live
according to the spirit of God and not the spirit of the flesh.

(Conference to the Daughters of Charity,
November 15, 1657- IX, 355 - ET: Leonard, III, 310)

Charity is a love above emotion and reason through which
people love one another to the same end Jesus Christ loved
people: to make them saints in this world and blessed in the
next.

(Abelly, 2d edition, 1667 - II, 106)

AFFECTIVE AND EFFECTIVE LOVE

*Each time Vincent spoke of the nature or the effects of the
love of God, he used the division of love into effective or
affective love which Francis de Sales used in his* Treatise on
the Love of God *and Saint Bernard before him.*

---

3. References to Leonard followed by a Roman and an Arabic numeral are
   to his translation, *The Conferences of Saint Vincent de Paul to the
   Sisters of Charity*, 4 vols. (Westminster, Md.: Newman Press, 1952).

Affective Love

Affective love is a certain flowing of the lover into the loved one, or the joy and tenderness a person has in the thing or person loved, like a father for his child.

(To Missionaries - XI, 43)

Affective love proceeds from the heart. The person who loves in this way is filled with sweetness and tenderness, is continually aware of the presence of God, finds satisfaction in thinking about God, and his or her life glides by insensibly in such contemplation. Thanks to this love, the soul accomplishes without pain, yes, with pleasure, the most difficult tasks and is vigilant and careful in regard to everything that may render it pleasing to God. Finally, it bathes in this divine love and takes no pleasure in any other thoughts. A father has two sons. One is still young. The father caresses him, plays with him, is delighted to hear him lisp, thinks of him when he does not see him, feels deeply his little sorrows. If he goes away from home the thought of his child is ever in his mind; when he returns he goes to see him first thing and loves him as Jacob loved his little Benjamin. There are some of you who love God truly, who feel great sweetness at prayer, great pleasure in all your spiritual exercises, great consolation in frequenting the sacraments, who experience no inner conflict, on account of the love you bear God who enables you to accept with joy and submission all that comes to you from his hand.

(Conference to the Daughters of Charity,
September 19, 1649 - IX, 475 - ET: Leonard, II, 101-02)

Affective love is the element of tenderness present in love. You should love our Lord tenderly and affectionately, like a child that cannot bear to be parted from its mother and cries out, "Mamma, Mamma," whenever she is about to leave it. Likewise a heart that loves our Lord cannot endure his ab-

sence, and owes it to itself to hold fast to him with this
affective love, which gives rise to effective love.

(To the Daughters of Charity, February 9, 1653
- IX, 593 - ET: Leonard, II, 204)

Effective Love

Effective love consists in doing the things that the person
we love wishes or orders, and it is of this kind of love the Lord
speaks when he says, "Whoever loves me will keep my word"
(Jn 14:15). This word consists of teachings and counsels. We
show our love by loving his teaching and publicly teaching it
to others. Consequently, the vocation of the Mission is a
vocation of love, for its concern is the doctrine and counsels
of Jesus Christ. It also commits itself to bringing the world to
esteem his doctrine and to love our Savior.

(Conference to Missionaries, XI, 43-44)

Love is effective when we act for God without feeling these
consolations. This love is not perceptible to the soul. The soul
does not feel it. Yet it produces its effect and accomplishes
its work.

A father has two sons. . . . One is still young. The other son
is a man of twenty-five or thirty years, his own master, who
goes where he pleases, returns home when he likes, and also
carries on the family business, and it seems as if the father
feels no tenderness for him and does not love him. If there is
any hard work, it is the son who will do it. If the father is a
farmer, it is the son who will have to look after everything
connected with work in the fields and help with it. If the
father is a merchant, the son will be engaged in trade. If the
father is a lawyer, the son will take care of the practice. And
to appearances the father has no love for his son.

But when it comes to making provision for him, the father
shows clearly that he loves him more than the little one whom
he so fondly caresses, for he gives the elder the best part of

his property and advances him plenty of money. We notice from the customs of certain countries that the eldest children are provided with the best part of the family's possessions, while the youngest have only a small portion by law. So it would seem that, although the father has a more tender and sensible love for the little one, he has a more effective love for the elder.

There are others among you who have no feeling for God at all. You have never felt him, you do not know what the meaning of sweetness at prayer is, you have no devotion, so you believe. Yet you do not cease to pray, to observe the rules, to practice virtue, to labor diligently, although with repugnance. Do you cease to love God? No, certainly not, for you do all that the others do and with a love that is all the stronger from the fact that you feel it less. This is effective love which does not cease to operate, although it does not make itself felt.

(To the Daughters of Charity, September 19, 1649
- IX, 475-477 - ET: Leonard, II, 216-17)

Superiority of Effective Love of God Over Affective Love

When our love stops at the invisible God without bearing fruit it is very easy to fall into an illusion that mistakes the idea, image, or desire of love for true charity.

Vague resolutions lead to illusion.

I am sending you Madame N's resolutions, which are good, but they would seem even better to me if she came down to particulars a little. It would be well to train the women who make their retreat exercises at your house to do that. All else is merely a product of the mind, which, because it has found some facility and even some sweetness in the consideration of a virtue, flatters itself into thinking that it is quite virtuous. Nevertheless, in order to become soundly virtuous, it is advisable to make practical resolutions concerning particular acts of the virtues and to be faithful in carrying them out afterwards. Without doing that, one is often virtuous only in one's imagination.

(Letter to Louise de Marillac, undated - ET: II, 216-17)

Today's reading in the refectory said that meditating on virtues without practicing them hurts us more than it helps us.

(To Jean Martin, November 14, 1658 - VII, 363-64)

Let us love God, my brothers, let us love God, but let it be in the strength of our arm and in the sweat of our brow. Sentiments of love of God, of kindness, of good will, good as these may be, are often suspect if they do not result in good deeds. Our Savior said that his Father was glorified in our bearing much fruit. We should be on our guard, for it is possible to be well mannered exteriorly and filled with noble sentiments toward the Almighty in our minds and yet stop there. When the occasion for action arises, such people fall short. They may be consoled by their fervent imagination or content with the sweet sentiments they experience in mental prayer. They may speak like the angels, but when it is a matter of working for God, of suffering, of mortifying themselves, of teaching the poor, of seeking out the lost sheep, of rejoicing at deprivations, of comforting the sick or some other service, here they draw the line. Their courage fails them. We must not deceive ourselves: all our work consists in action *(totum opus nostrum in operatione consisit).*

Monsieur Vincent often repeated these words, which he said he had first heard from the lips of a great servant of God on his deathbed when asked for some final edifying words. He had replied that he saw clearly in this last hour that what some people took as contemplation, ecstasy, or an overwhelming experience of God were not evidence of divine union but were mere smoke. This feeling proceeded from idle curiosity or the natural inclination of a mind inclined to the good. All this was far from good and perfect action which characterizes true love for God.

(Abelly, ET: I, 106-107)

Affective love which does not bear fruit is detrimental, the soul can be lost.

We see many who, however good their intentions and beautiful their resolutions, find themselves ineffective when it comes to implementing them or conquering difficulties. . . . Their pride forms a conscience which adapts to their sensuality. As a result nature takes the upper hand. I do not exaggerate. Experience shows it every day.

(To a Priest of the Mission, in 1647- ET:III, 163)

Uniting Affective and Effective Love

What then is the spirit of the Daughters of Charity? Sisters, it is the love of our Lord Jesus Christ. . . . And that you may understand what exactly this love is, you should know that it is exercised in two different ways, one affective, the other, effective. The first does not suffice. It is necessary to have both. Affective love must pass on to effective love which is the practice of the works of the Company of Charity, the service of the poor undertaken joyously, courageously, steadfastly and lovingly.

(To the Daughters of Charity, February 9, 1647
- IX, 593 - ET: Leonard, II, 204-205)

Uniting the Love of God and Neighbor

Our Lord Jesus Christ is the meek master of people and angels. By practicing this same virtue of meekness you will go to him and bring others to him as well.

(Abelly, ET: III, 168)

Jesus will not allow any union with himself, if there is none with those who represent him and with his members.

(To the Daughters of Charity,
April 24, 1647 - ET: III, 184)

Please embrace Father Portail for me, as I embrace all of you in spirit, begging our Lord to bind all of us together in his pure love, so that together we may love him uniquely, strongly, and eternally.

(Letter to Jean Martin, June 7, 1647 - ET: III, 203)

O Divine Goodness, unite all hearts in the Little Company of the Mission, then order whatever you please. Labors will be sweet to us and every task easy; the strong person will relieve the weak one, and the weak will cherish the strong and obtain increased strength for him from God. And so, Lord, your work will be done as you would like, for the building up of your Church, and your workers will multiply, attracted by the perfume of such charity.

(Letter to Etienne Blatiron, December 13, 1647 - ET: III, 258)

We are called . . . to separate ourselves from all that is not God and unite to our neighbor through charity in order to unite ourselves to God's own self through Jesus Christ.

(To the Missionaries, February 14, 1659 - XII, 127)

Humility

Presentation of Humility

Humility was the virtue which the Son of God in a very special way had engraved on his heart. His life was a fabric of humility and humiliations.

If I asked anyone among you to speak [on humility], no matter who he was, he would bring forward an abundance of authorities and motivations on this matter. I could bring forward some too. But to honor the words and sentiments of our Lord, we shall merely say that it has been recommended to us by himself. "Learn of me who am humble."

(To Missionaries, April 18, 1659 - XII, 196)

What is Jesus' life, Gentlemen, but a series of acts of humility? It is one of continual humiliation, active and passive. He loved humility to such an extent that he never left it while on earth. Not only did he love it during his life, but after his precious death he left an imperishable memorial of the humiliations of his divine person in the crucifix, appearing on it as a criminal attached to an ignominious cross. It was his will that the Church should place him before our eyes in the state of ignominy in which he died for us. It was his will that our benefactor should be set before us as a wicked man and that the author of life should suffer the most disgraceful and ignominious death. O my Savior! What love for this virtue! You delivered yourself to these extreme humiliations? Ah! You knew the excellence of this virtue and the malice of the sin opposed to it, which not only increases the guilt of other sins but vitiates works which in themselves are not evil and even those that are good, no, even the most holy.

(To Missionaries, April 18, 1659 - XII, 200)[4]

He emptied himself, so we could be like him.

My God! My Brothers, the time has come when his Divine Goodness causes us to speak on humility. Let us all, then, most humbly entreat him to grant us the grace of participating in his humility, and of practicing it like Jesus who practiced it unceasingly. How happy shall we be if what St. Paul said of our Lord in his humiliations may be said of each of us, "he humbled himself, taking the form of a slave."

---

4. The conference on humility from which this excerpt and those which follow have been taken can be read in its entirety in English in Joseph Leonard's translation, *Conferences of Saint Vincent de Paul* (Philadelphia, 1963), 526-540.

Eternal Father! You have willed that your Son be clothed with our flesh to be made like us, "he was made in human likeness and found clothed as a human being." Clothe us with the virtue of humility, that we may be like him.

(To Missionaries, April 18, 1659 - XII, 200-01)

Humility is the work of the Spirit of God. Grace alone leads to humility. Nature is inclined to pride and self.

Yes, Gentlemen, strange to say, when visiting or hearing confessions I have asked people, "What virtue do you most desire? To what do you have the greatest attraction?" I have noticed nearly all answered humility. "It is a virtue," each one said to me, "for which I have great affection, and still, though I love it, I cease not to be full of pride; by this am I troublesome to others whom I place below me; by this am I insupportable to myself by wishing to exalt myself as I do." Where does this come from? Even though we naturally have an inclination to pride, we have at the same time an inclination to humility, because it is beautiful to think about, or at least . . . because we would like to have this virtue. And how has that come about? It is because the grace received in baptism gives us this longing. Yes, the Spirit of our Lord gives the same tendency to virtue as nature does to vice.

(April 18, 1659 - XII, 197)

The Lord speaks to the heart.

Who shall be able to speak of the virtue of humility? O my Lord! Do us the favor of speaking to us yourself on this subject! Human words strike the ear and do not penetrate to the interior, but a single word of yours spoken to our hearts will make us renounce vainglory, by which the greater part of humanity loses the merit of their actions. Many of their actions are good in appearance but full of the hot air of self-esteem, which deprives them of weight and consistency and causes them to evaporate like smoke.

You know, my God, that the renouncement of honor is so painful, so contrary to nature, that if you do not speak to our hearts, we will never renounce it as we should. Speak to us, then, O Lord! Speak to us yourself. Behold us as so many servants attentive to your words.

(April 18, 1659 - XII, 201)

Humility is radically opposed to the spirit of the world.

My brothers, humility is so contrary to the spirit of the world and its maxims, so remote from the inclinations of people and from the heart of each individual, that if God had not spoken of it and accomplished it, no one would wish to hear it mentioned. People have so much esteem for what they possess and what they produce externally, that there is not even one who by nature does not wish to be of some repute and who does not strain every nerve to be praised and esteemed. Through a certain disposition of our nature spoiled by our first parents, we all succumb to this harmful tendency and fall into this miserable trap.

(To Missionaries, April 18, 1659 - XII, 197)

Humility looks to reality, truth, and God alone.

Humility has this peculiar property, that it hinders us from aiming at any esteem but yours, O my God, who give to things their proper value. Human beings do not know their true value. Is not the role of a fool to prefer the esteem of the world to yours, the shadow to the substance, a lie to the truth?

(To Missionaries, April 18, 1659 - XII, 211)

A Motive for Humility

The weight of sin in human life.

What can we expect from human weakness? What effect can nothing have? What can sin perform, and what else are

we than sin? If then each considers himself attentively, he will
see that he deserves contempt, not only in some things, but
generally in all. Let us hold for certain, Gentlemen, that in all
things we deserve contempt and are always contemptible by
reason of the opposition which is in us to the being and
sanctity of God, and our estrangement from the life and
actions of Jesus Christ. What convinces us of this truth is the
natural and continual bent we have toward evil and our
impotence for good. It is our experience that, even when we
believe we have succeeded in our actions and given wise
counsel and our helpful admonitions, we discover it is the
opposite that has happened with us.

(To Missionaries, April 18, 1659 - XII, 207)

Results Brought About By Humility

What is good takes place through humility.

If you ever hear of any good done by the Company, you
will see that it is because there was some trace of humility in
it, some plain and down-to-earth action, such as instructing
the peasants and serving the poor. If the candidates for
ordination leave this house edified (as they have), it is always
because of the humble and simple way of acting they see here.
One of them from the last ordination retreat left a note saying
how touched he had been by the humility he noticed in the
house.

(To Missionaries, April 18, 1659 - XII, 204)

Humility gives birth to and nourishes all the virtues.

Humility brings to the soul all of the other virtues. Whenever we humble ourselves, we go from being sinners to
pleasing God. Even if we were criminals, humility would
transform us into just people. On the other hand, even if we
were angels and possessed all of the virtues except humility,
the lack of humility would take them all away, and we would

become like the damned who have no virtues. No matter how charitable a person is, if he is not humble, he does not have charity and, without charity, even if he had enough faith to move mountains, gave his goods to the poor and his body to fire, all would be useless.

(To Missionaries, April 18, 1659 - XII, 210)

It ensures a right intention.

Humility has this characteristic that it prevents us from aiming at any esteem except that of yours, my God, who give all things their proper value. We do not know their true value.

(To Missionaries, April 18, 1659 - XII, 211)

Corporate Humility

The corporate humility of the first disciples.

Our Lord was not only humble in his own person but also in his Little Society. He drew together a few poor men, unpolished, without learning or good manners, who did not agree among themselves, who all abandoned him in the end, but who, after his death, were treated as he had been and were banished, despised, accused, condemned and put to death. Let us assist each other, then, my brothers, that we may all share in their humiliation, they who were the first to receive the instruction and example of the Master concerning this virtue. Let us not be ashamed to follow them. It is the Master himself who still speaks to us. At this moment he says to us, as he said to them, "Learn of me who am meek and humble of heart." Do as you have seen me do, for, from the first moment of my life to its close, I have taught you the practice of humility. That is what I have always taught you.

(To Missionaries, April 18, 1659 - XII, 205)

Corporate humility has three aspects:
- the first is to consider ourselves truly worthy of contempt;

- the second is to be happy others know our faults and despise them in us;
- the third is to hide, if possible, the good that God does through us and in us, in keeping with our own littleness, and rather to credit it to his mercy and the merits of others.

(April 18, 1659 - XII, 195)

Corporate humility includes accepting an undeserved bad reputation.

It is good that each one of us loves to be humble, but this is not enough. We must likewise have an affection for humility regarding the Congregation. Not only must we accept the humiliations that touch each one in particular but also those that touch all of us in general. We ought to be pleased to have it said that the Congregation is useless to the Church, that it is composed of poor beings, that whatever it does it does badly, that its missions in the country are performed without fruit, that its seminaries are without grace and its ordinations without order. My brothers, if we have the spirit of God, we will be pleased that the Congregation has the kind of reputation I just described and that it be ranked below all other congregations, rather than to want wonderful things said of it, or have its accomplishments known, or have great people esteem it or the bishops have a good opinion of it. Oh! May God preserve us from this folly!

(To Missionaries, April 18, 1659 - XII, 203)

A Portrait of Humble Missionaries

Humility as our identity and password.

I wish it were lawful for us, Gentlemen, from this day forward to take humility as the mark of a Missioner, so that we would be distinguished from ordinary Christians and from other priests by this virtue more than by our own name! May our Lord grant us this grace which corresponds to our state! Let us beg of him that, if we are asked what our state of life is, he may allow us to answer: "It is humility." Let this be our particular virtue. If we hear the question: "Who goes there?" let our password be "humility."

(To Missionaries, April 18, 1659 - XII, 206)

Humility creates a climate of peace, joy, and simplicity.

I must confess that I never meet certain persons without feeling deeply challenged and unnerved. They are a silent reproach to my pride. These poor people are always at peace, their joy shines on their faces. The Holy Spirit dwells in them, blessing them with his gift of peace so that nothing is able to trouble them. If they are contradicted, they give way. If calumniated, they bear it. If forgotten, they assume that it is with good reason. If they are overwhelmed with duties, they work willingly, doing whatever they can. The more difficult a command is, the more willingly they accept it, confiding in the power of holy obedience. Temptations which come to them serve only to strengthen their humility, making them have recourse to God and bringing them victories over the devil.

They have no further enemies to combat except pride, which makes truce with no one during life, but attacks even the greatest saints in various ways. It causes some to take vain complacency in the good they have done, or has others rejoice in the knowledge they have acquired. One missionary assumes he is especially enlightened, while another thinks of himself as better and more stable than others.

(To Missionaries, Abelly, ET: III, 201)

Iconography

A complete catalog of Vincentian iconography would include more than four thousand items. Thanks to the patient perseverance of Father Raymond Chalumeau, C.M., it is possible to discern the major lines in the development of Vincent's image. The purpose of the following classification is to help us keep our bearings among so many portraits and pictures and, ultimately, to help us see with a keen eye.

The Portraits of the Seventeenth century

We can rely on the portraits of the seventeenth century as the most faithful. The first is without doubt the one made by Simon François de Tours. The Vincentian Motherhouse has one which, if not the original, is at least a copy that belonged to Queen Anne of Austria. Starting with the sketches made by Simon François representing Saint Vincent, one in street clothes and the other in his surplice, four artists successively put themselves to the task: Nicholas Pitau, in 1660; Pierre Van Schuppen, in 1663; Réné Lochon, in 1664; Gerard Edelinck, in 1700.

The portrait of Vincent found in Saint-Etienne-du-Mont Church in Paris and dated 1649 has been attributed to Sebastian Bourdon, but the evidence is not decisive. The one of Angelique Labory in the birthplace of Vincent near Dax (Le Bercean) and dated 1654 probably dates from the nineteenth century.

In the Eighteenth Century

A. Portraits, paintings, engravings and statues

1. Gaspard Duchange did portraits of Vincent and Louise de Marillac in 1704 which are now kept in the Motherhouse of the Congregation of the Mission in Paris.

2. The beatification and canonization of Vincent inspired painters to do large tableaux.

a. Jean François de Troy (Paris, 1679-1742): **Saint Vincent preaching at the Court** (the original is in the Church of Saint Pierre in Macon; a copy is in the Presbytery of Saint-Eustachius in Paris); **Saint Vincent assisting Louis XIII at his death** (original was in Dresden in 1939; a nineteenth-century copy is at the Vincentian Motherhouse in Paris); **Saint Vincent at the Council of Conscience** (a nineteenth-century copy is at the Vincentian Motherhouse); **Saint Vincent and the Tuesday Conferences of Ecclesiastics** (the original was in Dresden in 1939); **The death of Saint Vincent**.

b. Brother André Jean, O.P. (Paris, 1662-1753): **The Glorification of Saint Vincent** (now at the Church of Bourg-la-Reine); **Saint Vincent preaching at the Hospice of the Name of Jesus** (now at the Church of Sainte-Marguerite de Paris; a copy is in the Vincentian Motherhouse).

c. Jean Restout, son. (Rouen, 1692-1753, Paris): **Saint Vincent appointed Superior of the Visitation Sisters by Francis de Sales** (now at the Church of Sainte-Marguerite de Paris); **Saint Vincent de Paul Chaplain General of the Galleys** (original lost).

d. Baptiste Feret (Evreux, 1737): **Saint Vincent sending his Missionaries and the Daughters of Charity to assist the wounded soldiers** (now at the Church of Sainte-Marguerite de Paris).

e. Galloche Louis (Paris, 1670-1761): **The Sermon of Saint Vincent concerning the Children Found in the Streets** (now at the Church of Sainte-Marguerite de Paris; a smaller copy is at the Presbytery of Saint-Eustachius).

f. Jacques Antoine Beaufort (Paris, 1721-1784, Rueil): **The miracles of Saint Vincent**.

g. Gaetan Sontin: **The Vision of the globes**.

B. To these paintings of great quality, all hanging in the Chapel of old Saint-Lazare before 1789, let us add two compositions.

1. Jean Restout: **Saint Vincent preaching** (dating back to 1739, kept at the Church of Notre-Dame de Versailles).

2. Noel Hall, brother-in-law of Jean Restout: **Saint Vincent preaching** (1761, now found in the Cathedral of Saint-Louis in Versailles).

C. The Prints of Robert Bonnard (born in 1683) popularized the tableaux of the beatification and canonization. It was also a Bonnard, namely Robert's uncle, Nicolas, who did the actual portrait of Louise de Marillac, that was later included by Gobillon in her first biography (Paris, 1676).

D. The statues of Vincent began to show up about the time of the beatification. One of the first, if not the very first, can be found today adorning the altar at Chaumont Hospital. Bracci did the statue for Saint Peter of Rome. The one sculpted by Stouf is presently at the Hospice des Enfants Assistés.

Bibliographic Essay

Saint Vincent de Paul is the subject of more than ten thousand books and articles. This abundance of published material attests to his influence. The following comments will acquaint readers with Vincent's writings as well as with those works of which he is the subject.

I. The Writings and Conferences of Saint Vincent de Paul

A. *Rules*. *Regulae seu Constitutiones Communes Congregationis Missionis* (*Common Rules and Constitutions of the Congregation of the Mission*). Paris, 1658. This was reprinted in 1672, sometime after 1737, in 1743 (Lisbon), in 1855 and in 1902.

B. *Correspondence*. It is estimated that Vincent wrote approximately thirty thousand letters. During the first two centuries after Vincent's death, the letters were used sparingly by his biographers. Abelly used two hundred of them (1664) and Collet referred to 250 (1748). In 1860, J. B. Pemartin published seven hundred letters and fragments of signed letters in *Receuil des diverses Exhortations et Lettres de Saint Vincent aux Missionaires* (*Selection of the Various Exhortations and Letters of Saint Vincent to the Missionaries*). Paris: Pillet and Dumoulin, 1860. In 1880 four volumes containing 2,039 letters were published in Paris by Pillet and Dumoulin. A supplement, published in 1888, contained one hundred more.

Between 1920 and 1925 Pierre Coste published 2,526 letters and excerpts of letters in the first eight volumes of *Saint Vincent de Paul, Correspondance, Entretiens, Documents*. 14 vols. Paris: Gabalda. This critical edition has been translated into Italian and Spanish. The English translation (*Saint Vincent de Paul, Correspondence, Conferences, Documents*. Brooklyn, N.Y.: New City Press, 1985 -) is in progress. A fifteenth volume containing correspondence located after 1925 was published in 1960.

C. *Conferences to the Daughters of Charity.* Volume IX and X of Coste (cited above) contains 120 conferences. The Daughters of Charity in Paris published a compact edition in 1952. Father Joseph Leonard's translation in English appeared in 1952 (*The Conferences of Saint Vincent de Paul to the Sisters of Charity.* 4 vols. Westminster, Md.)

D. *Conferences and Conversations with the Missionaries.* Volumes XI and XII of Coste (cited above) contains 224 conferences or informal talks. A more complete edition, with a critical introduction by André Dodin, was published by Editions du Seuil in 1960 under the title *Saint Vincent de Paul: Entretiens Spirituels à ses Missionaires (Saint Vincent de Paul, Spiritual Conferences to his Missionaries).* Father Joseph Leonard's translation in English appeared in 1963. (*Conferences of Saint Vincent de Paul.* Philadelphia: Eastern Province, U.S.A.).

II. Biographies

Four major biographical works have been published during the first three centuries after the death of Vincent. Because each draws from different sources, is written from a distinct perspective and with diverse objectives, the results are four original and complementary portraits.

A. Louis Abelly. *La Vie du Vénérable Serviteur de Dieu, Vincent de Paul. (The Life of the Venerable Servant of God, Vincent de Paul).* Paris: F. Lambert, 1664. The author of this three-volume work was a renowned theologian and a prolific spiritual writer. Although he was acquainted with Vincent as early as 1635, their twenty-two year association did not begin until 1638. Vincent's high regard for Abelly prompted him to recommend to the Bishop of Bayonne that he be appointed General Vicar and, eventually, Bishop of Rodez.

The priests of the Mission requested that Abelly write Vincent's biography. They placed at his disposal the archives of the Mission, its reports and the archives of the Daughters of Charity. Abelly recast these materials in the literary style of his era and his work remained the official biography in use by the Congregation of the Mission and the Company of the Daughters of Charity until 1748. It was the only document in which one could adequately know Vincent's identity, the esteemed and gracious spirit in which he moved and an illustration of the Rule of Missionaries and practical commentary on the gospels.

Abelly's work has been published in seventeen French editions. Five additional editions of Noiret's summary (Paris: 1929) were published during the years prior to Vincent's canonization, 1729-1736. The Italian translation was begun in 1677 and became the source for the Polish (1688), Spanish (1701) and German (1710) editions. Abelly's work has also appeared in Dutch and, in 1993, in English (New City Press).

B. Pierre Collet, C.M. (1693-1770). *La Vie de Saint Vincent de Paul* (*The Life of Saint Vincent de Paul*). Nancy, 1748.

Pierre Collet, like Abelly, was a theologian and priest of the Mission. He drew upon the documents prepared for Vincent's beatification and canonization. With great fidelity to his sources, Collet organized his work chronologically. It lacks literary grace but became a biographical documentary of the evidence for Vincent's canonization. Collet's "Summaries," which proliferated after 1762, were used as the basis for all popular biographies of Vincent published during the nineteenth century.

More than seventy editions of the *Life* and its summaries have been published over the course of three centuries. In addition, they have appeared in Italian, Spanish, and English. The image of Vincent is matter-of-fact and unaffected.

C. Michèl Ulysse Maynard. *Saint Vincent de Paul, sa vie, son temps, son influence* (*Saint Vincent de Paul, His Life, Times and His Influence*). Paris, 1860.

Canon Maynard devoted ten years to the writing of the *Biographie du IIe centenaire* (*The Biography of the Second Centenary*). Maynard, an astute and cultivated professor of rhetoric, wrote with clarity, precision and eloquence. He relied upon the archives and library of the Vincentian Motherhouse, and his four-volume work enjoyed much success. Vincent's faithful followers believe it has no parallel or equal. Six editions were issued between 1860 and 1886, and translations have appeared in Polish, Italian, Latin, Dutch, German and English. Maynard's gift was to present Vincent's works in their historical development and integrity. He did not treat the relationship between these works and the economic, literary and spiritual milieu, which, in fact, received little attention in those days. The result, however, was a portrait of a hero isolated from his times. As a consequence, Vincent's rich and profound humanity was overlooked.

D. Pierre Coste, C.M. (1873-1935) published *Le Grand Saint du Grand Siècle, Monsieur Vincent* (*The Great Saint of the Great Century*) in 1932, 3 vols. (Paris: Gabalda).

He is the first of Vincent's biographers to make use of the entire collection of Vincent's available writings and documentary materials. Father Francis Verdier, Superior General of the Mission, praised Coste, "It is unlikely that new discoveries would modify the profile that you present of your hero."

Coste, more an archivist than a historian, presents an impressive documentary which is weakened, however, by its neglect of the substance of Vincent's spirituality. For all Coste's painstaking efforts, he fails to show Vincent within his historical milieu. Vincent appears immune to the mood of the seventeenth century. This is an example of the type of biography which documents but does not enliven history.

Coste's work has been a gold mine for subsequent biographers. His documentation was invaluable and they were able to present it in a more engaging fashion. For instance:

La Vraie Vie de Saint Vincent de Paul (*The True Life of Saint Vincent de Paul*), by Antoine Rédier (1927);

Saint Vincent de Paul, by Paul Renaudin (1927); and *Monsieur Vincent, Aumônier Général des Galères* (*Monsieur Vincent, General Chaplain of the Galleys*), published in 1928 by Henri Lavedan.

Saint Vincent de Paul, by Vincent Giraud (Paris, 1932).

Remarkable for its literary quality is Jean Calvet's biography, *Saint Vincent de Paul* published in 1948. It has been published in Spanish, Italian and English, *Saint Vincent de Paul* (New York: David Mc Kay, 1951). Its companion volume is *Portrait de Louise de Marillac* (Editions Montaigne, 1958), translated in English as *Louise de Marillac: A Portrait* (New York: P.J. Kenedy, 1959).

E. Recent Editions. During the past thirty years, there has been considerable work on the life of Vincent. The following biographies are representative of this renewed effort.

St. Vincent de Paul, by Leonard von Matt and Louis Cognet (Chicago, 1960).

Monsieur Vincent: The Story of St. Vincent de Paul, by Henri Daniel-Rops (London, 1961).

The World of Monsieur Vincent, by Mary Purcell (London and New York, 1963; reprinted Dublin: Veritas, 1989).

San Vicente de Paúl, Volume I: Biografia, by José Maria Roman (Madrid, 1981). It is being translated into English at present and is expected to appear in the near future. The companion volume is *San Vicente de Paúl, Volume II: Espiritualidad y selección de escritos*, by Antonino Orcajo y Miguel Perez Flores (Madrid, 1981).

San Vincenzo de Paul: una carità senza frontiere, by Luigi Mezzadri (Torino, 1986). *A Short Life of Saint Vincent de Paul.* (Dublin: Columba Press, 1992).

III. Special Studies

Monographs dedicated to a particular apostolate, institute or regional activity multiplied during the nineteenth century. These studies reveal an emerging historical sense and, on the whole, are well done. They rely upon public documents and archival materials. The following sample gives a sense of these studies.

A. Political and social history:

Alphonse Feillet, *La Misère au Temps de la Fronde et Saint Vincent de Paul* (*The Misery During the Fronde and Saint Vincent de Paul*). Paris, 1862. Reprinted in 1864, 1865, 1868.

B. History of Institutions:

Pierre Coste, C.M., *Saint Vincent et les Dames de Charité* (*Saint Vincent and the Ladies of Charity*). Paris, 1917.

Arthur Loth, *Saint Vincent de Paul et sa Mission Sociale* (*Saint Vincent de Paul and his Social Mission*). Paris, 1880. Reprinted in 1881 and 1906. Spanish, 1887.

C. Aspects of Vincent's Activities:

Gaston Parturier: *La Vocation Médicale de Saint Vincent de Paul* (*The Medical Vocation of Saint Vincent de Paul*). Lyon, 1943.

IV. Studies of Vincent's Spirituality

Historians have been captivated by Vincent's deeds but have paid little attention to his spiritual experience and doctrine. Because public access to his letters and conferences had been limited, research and reflection were not possible.

A. *Seeking the Spirit of Vincent.* The Vincentian tradition, beginning during his lifetime and continuing through our era, has given much attention to its institutional dimensions. It has been slow, however, to give attention to the spirit of Vincent himself. Abelly (1664) and Collet (1748) merely alluded to his unique spirit. On the eve of the French Revolution, André Joseph Ansart gathered and distilled the familiar themes of Vincent's teachings. The timeliness and success of his *L'Esprit de Saint Vincent de Paul* (*The Spirit of Saint Vincent de Paul*) is attested by the publication of seven French editions (1780-1852) as well as Spanish, German, Dutch, Polish and English translations.

B. *Nineteenth Century.* Canon Maynard's *Vertus et Doctrine Spirituelle de Saint Vincent de Paul* (Paris, 1864) (*Virtues and Spiritual Doctrine of Vincent de Paul*), which was written for general readers, met with great success. During the sixty years immediately following publication, eleven new editions were released. The book continued to enjoy success in English, German, Dutch, Italian, Chinese and Spanish.

C. *A New Era.* The publication of the complete works of Saint Vincent de Paul (1920-25) began a new era.

Father G. Arnaud D'Agnel introduced Vincent as a pastor in *Saint Vincent de Paul, Directeur de Conscience* (*Saint Vincent de Paul, Spiritual Director*). Paris, 1925; *Saint Vincent de Paul, Guide du Prêtre* (*Saint Vincent de Paul, Guide of Priests*); and *Saint Vincent de Paul, Maître d'Oraison* (*Saint Vincent de Paul, Master of Prayer*). Paris, 1929.

Pierre Deffrennes, S.J., undertook to define Vincent's spiritual doctrine in "La Vocation Surnaturelle de Saint Vincent de Paul" ("The Supernatural Vocation of Saint Vincent de Paul"), *Revue d'Ascétique et de Mystique* 13 (1932) 60-86; 164-183; 294-321; 389-411.

Louis Deplanque, *Saint Vincent de Paul sous l'Emprise Chrétienne* (*Saint Vincent de Paul Under the Christian Vision*), (Literature dissertation, Paris, 1936) catalogues Vincent's teachings.

Siiri Juva probes Vincent's life with techniques derived from psychoanalysis. Her findings are reported in *Monsieur Vincent, Evolution d'un Saint* (*Monsieur Vincent, Evolution of a Saint*). Bourges, 1939.

Jacques Delarue, in his doctoral thesis in theology, was able to distill the constant elements of Vincent's teachings regarding priesthood, *L'Idéal Missionaire du Prêtre, D'aprés Saint Vincent de Paul* (*The Ideal Missionary Priest According to Saint Vincent de Paul*) Paris, 1947. The Southern Province, U.S.A., made a typescript of Joseph Leonard's translation available c. 1985. An edition of Joseph Lilly's translation is in progress. See also, Jacques Delarue's *The Holiness of Vincent* (New York, 1960).

Also worthy of mention is Jesus Maria Muneta's *La Espiritualidad de San Vicente de Paúl* (*The Spirituality of Saint Vincent de Paul*). Madrid, 1956.

D. *Vincent's Spiritual Way*. In none of these works is there a systematic examination of Vincent's spiritual experience, his spiritual development or the sources of his spiritual doctrine. Research in this direction has begun. See, for example, André Dodin, "Lectures de Saint Vincent de Paul" ("Reading Saint Vincent de Paul") in the *Annales de le Congrégation de la Mission*, 106-07 (1941-42) 239-48; 110-11 (1945-46) 447-64; 112-13 (1947-48) 479-97; "Saint Vincent de Paul et les Illuminés" ("Saint Vincent de Paul and the Enlightened") *Revue d'Ascétique et de Mystique* 25 (1949) 445-56; and especially, the Introduction to *Saint Vincent de Paul* (Paris: Aubier, 1949), pages 7-31.[1] Other themes treated by the author concern the promotion of women in the missionary apostolate,

---

1. Editor's note: these few pages are a masterly synthesis of Vincent's spiritual experience and spiritual doctrine.

Vincent as a mystic of religious action, Vincent's spirit as the spirit of the Mission, his humanism and his theology of charity (see the French edition for the bibliographic references). These studies reveal a new approach to Vincent and open up new vistas.

E. *Mission to the Poor*. Since the Second Vatican Council's call to the renewal of religious communities through the charism of the founder, intensive study and reflection on the evangelization and service of the poor has taken place throughout the Vincentian family. A significant example of this research is found in José Maria Ibañez, *Vicente de Paùl y los pobres de su tiempo* (Salamanca, 1977) and the recent publication in English of Jacques Bénigne Bossuet's sermon "On the Eminent Dignity of the Poor in the Church," by Edward Udovic, C.M. in *Vincentian Heritage* 13 (1992) 37-58. Finally, Father Robert P. Maloney, the present Superior General of the Congregation of the Mission, has published *The Way of Vincent de Paul: A Contemporary Spirituality in the Service of the Poor* (New City Press, 1991).

F. *Organized Study*. The study and promotion of the charism of Vincent has been organized at the international and national levels and has year by year been coming to maturity.

SIEV (The International Secretariat for Vincentian Studies) organized and presented international seminars for Vincentian priests and brothers in 1981, 1984, 1987 and 1990. These sessions came to be known as "The Vincentian Month." The papers of the first session were published as a separate volume, *Vincent de Paul: Actes du Colloque International d'Etudes Vincentiennes, Paris, 25-26 septembre 1981* (Roma: Edizione Vincenziane). The subseqeunt three were published in the *Vincentiana*, which is the official commentary for member of the Congregation of the Mission. See volumes 28 (1984), 31 (1987) and 34 (1990).

Two English language periodicals, recently founded, are making a steady contribution to the knowledge of Vincentian history and, to some extent, to reflection on the contemporary challenge. They are *Colloque: Journal of the Irish Province of the Congregation of the Mission* (1979-); and *Vincentian Heritage* (1980-), published jointly by the Congregation of the Mission and the Daughters of Charity of the Provinces of the U.S.A.

Two recent bibliographies are of invaluable assistance to anyone who wishes to delve further into the spirit of Vincent. They are *Biblioteca Vincenciana de la casa central de los Padres Paules, Madrid: Catalogo Sistematico* (Madrid, 1988) by José Maria Roman, C.M. and Carlos Corcuera, C.M. and, in English, "Saint Vincent de Paul: Bibliography to 1991," *Vincentian Heritage*, 12 (1991) no. 1, pp. 51-78 by John Rybolt, C.M.

The final word goes to Father Dodin who has just published the comments of one of Saint Vincent's two secretaries, Louis Robineau, *Monsieur Vincent raconté par son Secrétaire* (Paris, 1991), which gives an intimate and daily feeling for Vincent.